THE FULL
ARMOR
OF GOD

THE FULL ARMOR OF GOD

DEFENDING YOUR LIFE FROM SATAN'S SCHEMES

LARRY RICHARDS, Ph.D.

Chosen

a division of Baker Publishing Group
Minneapolis, Minnesota

© 2013 by Lawrence O. Richards

Published by Chosen Books
11400 Hampshire Avenue South
Bloomington, Minnesota 55438
www.chosenbooks.com

Chosen Books is a division of
Baker Publishing Group, Grand Rapids, Michigan

Printed in the United States of America

Library of Congress Cataloging-in-Publication Data
Richards, Larry.
    The full armor of God : defending your life from Satan's schemes / Larry Richards.
        p. cm.
    Summary: "Accessible, practical guide from Ephesians shows how to defend yourself and your loved ones from Satan's schemes by putting on the whole armor of God"—Provided by publisher.
    ISBN 978-0-8007- 9542-9 (pbk. : alk. paper)
    1. Spiritual warfare—Biblical teaching. 2. Bible. N.T. Ephesians—Criticism, interpretation, etc. I. Title.
BS680.S73R53 2013
235'.4—dc23   2012040229

Cover design by Kirk DouPonce, DogEared Design

13 14 15 16 17 18 19   7 6 5 4

Contents

Preface

Ephesians was written to young believers in the city of
Ephesus, the first city in Asia. Ephesus boasted the Temple of Diana, Asia Minor's premier deity, and was visited
annually by thousands of pilgrims. But Ephesus, like the rest
of the first-century world, was filled with people who were uncertain about their future and fearful that their fate was in the
hands of powers over which they had no control. Every resident
of Ephesus sensed what Paul meant when he wrote that "our
struggle is not against flesh and blood, but against the rulers,
against the authorities, against the powers of this dark world
and against spiritual forces of evil in the heavenly realms."

Today we Christians are less aware than first-century believers that there is an invisible war between God and Satan going
on around us. Yet we, too, struggle with uncertainty, fears and
doubts. Scripture makes it clear that much of our self-doubt,
much of our difficulty in maintaining satisfying personal relationships and many of the fears that trouble us are rooted in
the efforts of those same "spiritual forces of evil" that plagued
the Ephesians. That is why it is so vital that we understand the

message of the Bible's book of Ephesians. In Ephesians the apostle Paul unveils the strategies Satan uses to attack believers. And he also explains the armor that God has provided to shield us from Satan's attacks.

In this book we are going to examine each piece of God's armor in sequence as Paul treats it and see exactly how we can put that armor on. I am convinced that this can launch you on a journey that will bring you more freedom and more joy than you have experienced in your Christian life. In using the resources that God provides, you truly will be shielded from Satan's efforts to make your life empty and unfulfilling. You will know how to defend your life from the enemy's most powerful schemes.

This book includes much that I teach in the Freedom Workshops I conduct around the country at no charge. While it is impossible to re-create here the experience of participating in a Freedom Workshop, this book will help you understand God's provision. And the exercises I include will help you experience His freedom.

If you would like to schedule a Freedom Workshop in your church or community, please contact me at ancient1@nc.rr.com.

Larry Richards

PART 1

UNDERSTANDING SPIRITUAL FORCES

1

Spiritual Forces of Evil Then

In A.D. 53 the apostle Paul approached the city of Ephesus. He was traveling along a major Roman road known locally as "the common highway." Leaving a broad plain, the highway mounted a ridge, and from its top Paul caught the first glimpse of his destination. The city of Ephesus was hidden behind a wall seven meters high, but from the ridge Paul could see the Artemision, the temple of the goddess Artemis (also known as Diana), which lay just south of the city proper. The magnificent temple, its columns glowing in the light of the sun, was hailed even in that day as one of the seven wonders of the world.

The Artemision was an appropriate possession of the city, for, in the first century, Ephesus was the third most prominent city in the Roman Empire. Ephesus boasted a quarter of a million inhabitants. The city sat astride important land and sea trade routes, and was both the economic and religious center of the province of Asia. Ephesus was also the destination of thousands of religious pilgrims who flocked to the city each year to worship the goddess and seek her aid.

Paul, however, was not approaching Ephesus as a pilgrim. He was coming as a missionary, intent on spreading the Gospel of Jesus Christ. That mission would bring him into direct conflict with the "spiritual forces of evil in the heavenly realms" (Ephesians 6:12), for Ephesus was more than a center of pagan religion: It was also a center of demonic activity, a place where magic and sorcery were practiced in an effort to control the powerful spirits that people believed ruled their destinies.

During Paul's stay in Ephesus open conflict would erupt between Christ and demonic powers that owed their allegiance to Satan. And the powers would not surrender without a battle.

A Look at Acts 19

Luke's account of Paul's ministry in Ephesus, given in Acts 19, serves as an appropriate introduction to the New Testament book of Ephesians. Acts 19 also explains the emphasis in Ephesians on the believer's defense against demonic oppression. Note these features of the Acts 19 account.

First, Paul is described as casting out evil spirits and healing the sick (see Acts 19:11–12). These "extraordinary miracles" freeing victims of demonic oppression were performed in public. Everyone in the city knew of the apostle's actions.

Second, we are told of seven sons of Sceva, who were exorcists (see verses 13–16). In the first century, Jewish exorcists were held in high regard, for they were thought to know the secret name of the Jews' powerful deity and, thus, could enlist His aid. In those days, exorcism was performed by invoking the name of a powerful spirit—such as an angel, demon or deity—and placing that spirit under a spell. The spirit could then be directed to order out any lesser demon that was tormenting the victim.

But one day when the seven Jewish exorcists tried to invoke the name of Jesus in this way, the demonized man attacked and beat all seven. The evil spirit spoke, saying that it knew Jesus and knew about Paul, but recognized no authority in these seven men. Because they had no personal relationship with Jesus, they had no authority over evil spirits. When this event "became known to the Jews and Greeks living in Ephesus, they were all seized with fear, and the name of the Lord Jesus was held in high honor" (verse 17).

The third story in Acts 19 indicates how powerfully Paul's defeat of demons influenced the Christian community (see verses 18–20). Many who had practiced sorcery as a defense against demons brought out their books of spells and magic and burned them publicly. Luke tells us that the burned books were worth fifty thousand drachma, which represented fifty thousand days' worth of income!

Taken together these three stories make it very plain that Ephesus was a center of satanic activity. Thus, the Acts account provides an important clue to understanding the purpose and value of this significant New Testament epistle—for Ephesians has more references to demonic powers than any other New Testament letter, and Paul views its teaching as divinely provided armor against the attacks of evil spirits.

First-Century View of the Spirit World

In the first century, most people were well aware that the spirit world is real, and believed it to be occupied by a variety of spirits. There were spirits of the dead. There were spirits of the heroes of old. There were spirits who were gods and goddesses. And there were demons . . . evil spirits. All these spirits were believed to interact with the world of men and to have impact on the living. Everything—success in business, in love, in athletic competitions, even in one's health—depended on whether the spirits were pleased or displeased with an individual. And the spirits were at best capricious. None really cared about a human's welfare; any spirit was more likely to harm a person than help him. The best anyone could do was to make offerings to placate possibly angry or hostile spirits, or resort to magic to try to control them.

First-century Roman writer Plutarch notes that the sorcerers of his time advised those who were demonized to "recite and name over to themselves the Ephesians letters." These "letters" were six supposedly magic words that were written on separate pieces of leather, and could be shuffled and recited in differing order. If one order of the six words did not work, perhaps another order would—for even sorcery was not reliable.

No one in Ephesus had ever seen a person dominate demons as Paul did. No wonder the people of the city held Paul and the name of Jesus in such awe.

And no wonder, after Paul left the city and the young Christian Church, he wrote them a reassuring letter. In that letter, his epistle to the Ephesians, Paul made very plain how Christians can defend themselves against the attacks of evil spirits who are armed with strategies devised by Satan himself.

2

Spiritual Forces of Evil Now

What would Paul find if he approached a modern American city like Seattle, where I am as I write this? Seattle is an exciting city with its sea lanes touching the Pacific Rim. It is a prosperous city despite the current recession—the home of Google, Microsoft and important financial institutions. It boasts a fine art museum, fantastic mountain vistas and a major international airport.

It would not take the apostle Paul long, however, to realize that spiritual forces of evil are at work here. There are many churches, but most of the population is unchurched. In fact, the life of the pastor of one of the most vital churches in the community has been threatened so often that armed bodyguards attend all church services. According to research by the Pew organization, some 25 percent of people who attend evangelical churches hold pagan beliefs, such as a belief in reincarnation, and are unaware that these beliefs conflict with Christian teaching!

If this modern-day Paul were to turn on the television and scan the programs offered by the networks and cable channels, he would find that no fewer than sixty programs feature the supernatural—everything from A&E's *Paranormal State* to CBS's *Medium*. Satan is using the media to infiltrate American culture with pagan notions.

Many people are hooked on the occult—as shown by a quick look at www.Meetup.com, a website that helps people find and join interest groups. Punching in a Seattle area zip code, Paul would discover that within 25 miles of the city are some eleven shamanistic groups, with memberships ranging from 60 to 219. He would find ten Wiccan groups, such as the Greater Seattle Witches meetup, with 587 members, and he would find the 205-member Free Witches meetup.

If Paul checked further he would find twelve groups that seek supernatural guidance through reading tarot cards. He would find nine groups, like the Spirit Speaks meetup, that look to spirit guides to help them make choices. He would also find nine groups like the 101-member Psychic Reading and Energy Healing meetup. And, of course, he would see that the Seattle Pagan meetup claims 371 members, while the nearby Everett Pagan meetup claims 251. If Paul kept looking, he might run across the Witch School, an online institution with more than 227,000 regular students, many of whom are working toward ordination as a witch or warlock.

Such active involvement in the occult and fascination with the spirit world was uncommon just 25 years ago. American culture is changing, and with it the beliefs of the new generations.

What Is the Modern View of the Spirit World?

Strikingly, modern beliefs about the spirit world mirror the beliefs of the first century—notably that entities in the spirit world exert powerful influence over one's personal life. These entities include the spirits of dead relatives, of individuals from ancient times, of gods and goddesses, of angels and demons and even of spirits of animals (totems).

The major difference between the beliefs of many people today and the beliefs of first-century Ephesians lies in the fact that first-century men and women feared the spirits. Moderns assume that the spirits are well disposed to humans and eager to help. As a result moderns tend to be comfortable going to palm readers or clairvoyants, mediums or witches, or calling directly on spirits for help and guidance. When encouraged to invite a "spirit guide" into their lives, many unhesitatingly open the door to demons—for the spirits that modern pagans seek to contact are what the Bible identifies as demons!

What about Christians?

If Paul visited a modern American church, he would find that most Christians are completely ignorant of what is happening in our culture. He would also discover that most Christians have no idea of the impact the spirit world has on our lives—even for good. Oh, most of us assume that there are such things as guardian angels. But we are totally unaware of how angels might minister to us.

Paul would also learn that few Christians today take demons seriously. If pressed, most of us would say that we believe that Satan exists and that demons probably are real. But the notion that demons might be the cause of many of our spiritual, emotional and even physical problems is totally foreign to most of us Americans. And this is not surprising. Satan today tends to operate behind the scenes in our culture, rather than in the open, public conflict that occurred in Ephesus.

If we look in the Bible, we find only three time periods when the struggle against demons broke out into the open.

- *The time of the Exodus.* The plagues that God brought on Egypt were judgments on the gods of Egypt, who were demons presenting themselves as deities (see 1 Corinthians 10:20). The destruction brought by the miracles demonstrated the power of God over the demonic.

- *The time of Elijah and Elisha.* In the eighth century B.C., King Ahab imported the religion of Baal in an effort to supplant worship of Yahweh. Elijah and Elisha performed miracles that demonstrated "the Lord, He is God" (see 1 Kings 18:24).

- *The time of Jesus and the apostles.* In the first century, demonic activity increased as Satan marshaled his forces against the Messiah. Jesus, and later the apostles, publicly cast out demons and healed the sick.

Aside from these periods of open, public conflict with evil spirits, demons remain active, but hidden. Despite the fact that few witness open and obvious demonic activity in our culture today, demons remain active. But with demonic activity "behind the scenes," the tendency even among Christians is to discount their influence. Recognizing this tendency, Paul taught his followers and also left future generations a legacy enabling us to recognize and combat demons.

Recognition begins when we understand that real spiritual warfare takes place within the hearts and lives of individuals. Satan operates what Paul calls "schemes." These schemes, or strategies, are designed to cripple believers and to make them miserable and ineffective. Demons are always looking for an open door through which they can enter to oppress and cripple believers. Thus, chances are good that there are areas in every Christian's life where demonic oppression is robbing him or her of the freedom believers are intended to have in Christ.

Let's look more closely at the work of these forces of evil.

3

The Role of Demons

When the apostle Paul wrote to the Ephesians about the "spiritual forces of evil in heavenly realms" (Ephesians 6:12), he knew exactly what he was writing about. Ever since Satan showed up in Eden and manipulated Adam and Eve into declaring independence from God, dark forces have lurked behind the scenes of history, intent on causing as much suffering and misery as possible.

In Old Testament times, spiritual forces of evil found expression in the gods and goddesses who were worshiped by pagan peoples. According to Deuteronomy 32:16–17, the "foreign gods" of the nations around Israel were in reality demons. The Old Testament also refers to these dark forces as *evil spirits*, *perverse spirits*, *lying spirits*, *unclean spirits*, etc.

In the gospels, the spiritual forces of evil are called by the familiar terms *demons* or *evil spirits*. There we catch a glimpse of just how hostile demons are to human beings. Demons were responsible for a great number of mental and physical ills, from madness to blindness. They crippled human beings and were intent on causing pain and suffering. But in the gospel accounts, demons run into Jesus. And in every confrontation, the demons lose and are driven out of the individuals they oppress.

The New Testament epistles refer to demons using words common to Greek language and culture. Paul did call these spiritual forces of evil *demons* in 1 Corinthians 10:20 and 1 Timothy 4:1, but normally the New Testament letters refer to evil spirits in the vocabulary used by the average first-century citizen. In the first century, the man on the street called the inhabitants of the spirit world—that is, the gods and goddesses, the spirits of the dead, the angels and demons—by the names *principalities, rulers, powers, dominions, thrones, spiritual forces* or *elemental spirits*.

When the apostle Paul wrote in Ephesians that "our struggle is not against flesh and blood, but against the *rulers*, against the *authorities*, against the *powers* of this dark world and against the *spiritual forces* of evil in the heavenly realms" (Ephesians 6:12, emphasis added), everyone knew he was referring to evil spirits.

Demons, whose realm is the spirit world—the "heavenly realms"—really do mount attacks on humans living in this world.

What Are Demons?

Demons, while not flesh and blood, are personal beings. In my book *Every Good and Evil Angel in the Bible* (Nelson, 1998), I wrote,

> The Gospels use personal pronouns when reporting dialog with demons (see Luke 8:27–30); individual demons apparently have personal names, and groups of demons have "team" names (see Luke 8:30). Demons can communicate and hold conversations (see Luke 4:22–26; 8:28–30). Demons also have intelligence (see Mark 1:23–24; Luke 4:34; 8:28), emotions (see Luke 8:28) and

will (see Mark 1:27; Luke 4:35–36). So demons, while spirit beings, are individuals—persons—with their own individual identities.

Most Bible students believe that demons are angels who followed Satan when he rebelled against God. Matthew 25:41 refers to "Satan and his angels." Revelation 12:4 seems to suggest that about a third of the angels God created cast their lot with Satan and became demons.

Whatever the origin of demons, they clearly are allied with Satan. Demons are hostile to God and hate human beings. It is also clear that demons can "get inside" our personalities. When Jesus confronted a demon who was tormenting a human, the Bible describes Jesus as casting the demon *out*. To be thrown out, the demon must in some sense have been *in*!

So demons are evil spirits, hostile to us and eager to gain some kind of access to our lives so they can make us as miserable and unproductive as possible.

Shut the Doors

The apostle Paul refers to demons using the *principalities* and *powers* vocabulary in seven of his thirteen New Testament letters. In Ephesians he mentions *principalities, authorities, powers, dominions, world rulers* and *spiritual forces*, and, as I noted earlier, refers to them more often than in any of his other letters.

This emphasis in Ephesians should not surprise us. As we learned from looking at Acts 19, Ephesus was a center of magic and sorcery, a hive of demonic activity. It is natural that Paul would deal with demons in this letter to a church deeply engaged in the struggle against the "spiritual forces of evil in the heavenly realms." Moreover, Paul would want to teach these believers how to slam the doors shut against any possible invasion by demons.

And what is exciting is that in teaching the Ephesians how to stand against demonic attacks, Paul is also teaching you and me!

In fact, we can view the book of Ephesians as Paul's handbook on spiritual warfare. Ephesians is Paul's "freedom workshop," instructing us how to break free, and remain free, from the influence of evil spirits that are eager to infiltrate believers' lives.

One special note. The danger from demons is not being "demon possessed." The word *possessed* is not found in the gospels. The Greek word is *daimonizomai,* which simply means "demonized." Demons do not "possess" their victims, in the sense of gaining control.

What demons do is influence us. They tempt us, twist our thinking and cloud our understanding. They lie to us about our identity in Christ, telling us we are useless and hopeless. Demons encourage bitterness and anger and destroy healthy relationships. They stimulate our fears and cause panic. They drown us in depression and despair. They tell us that we cannot risk stepping out in faith to respond to God's Word. Demons push us toward addictions that can ruin our lives. And sometimes in the process demons ruin our health.

In all these ways demons can and do oppress believers. It is no wonder Paul uses one of his letters to spell out God's defense against demons. And to set God's people free.

4

Combating the Forces of Evil

The book of Ephesians has proven difficult for the writers of commentaries. Simply put, they cannot agree on what this brief letter is really about, or how to outline it. Everyone recognizes common themes. But it seems no one can agree with anyone else on how these themes fit together to make a unified whole. Only one book on Ephesians that I know of even comments that repeated references to *principalities* and *powers* play a central role in the book. Yet when we realize that Paul's whole letter is about combating spiritual forces of evil, the structure of Ephesians is easily discernible. Paul even points out the structure he uses near the end of the book.

The Armor of God

In the first century, the whole Mediterranean world was at peace. It was a peace imposed and maintained by Roman armies. And the key to this Roman military achievement was the heavily armored Roman legionnaire.

Infantrymen in the Roman legions were equipped with a standard suit of armor. Paul describes this armor in Ephesians 6, and draws an analogy between the pieces of the infantryman's armor and the spiritual armor God provides so that we can stand against demonic enemies that operate in the spiritual realm.

> Stand firm then, with the belt of truth buckled around your waist, with the breastplate of righteousness in place, and with your feet fitted with the readiness that comes from the gospel of peace. In addition to all this, take up the shield of faith, with which you can extinguish all the flaming arrows of the evil one. Take the helmet of salvation and the sword of the Spirit, which is the word of God.
>
> Ephesians 6:14–17

Notice that each piece of armor stands for a spiritual truth or resource.

Belt	=	Truth
Breastplate	=	Righteousness
Sandals	=	Preparation that comes from Gospel of peace
Shield	=	Faith
Helmet	=	Salvation

Then Paul tells us to take up the "sword of the spirit," and explains that the sword is "the Word of God." The sword is the only item that Paul defines, in part because the sword is an offensive weapon. Paul's focus is on defense against spiritual attack, not offense. But the basic reason that Paul identifies the sword and does not explain truth, righteousness, peace, faith or salvation here is that *these pieces of armor are fully explained throughout the letter he has just written!*

24

By observing one additional point, we find that the structure of the book of Ephesians is unveiled. In Ephesians 6, Paul lists the pieces of armor in the order in which the Roman legionnaire put the armor on. But in writing this letter *he deals with each piece of armor in reverse order.*

So now we can both outline Ephesians, and grasp the nature of the armor God provides—armor that enables us to slam the door on evil spirits and stand securely against them.

The Structure of the Book of Ephesians

Acts 19	Ephesians 1:1–23	Ephesians 2:1–10	Ephesians 2:11–4:16	Ephesians 4:17–5:7	Ephesians 5:8–6:9	Ephesians 6:10–24
Introduction to Ephesians	Helmet	Shield	Sandals	Breastplate	Belt	Summary
	Salvation	Faith	Peace	Righteousness	Truth	

Journey to Freedom

As I promised in the introduction, in this book we are going to examine each piece of God's armor in sequence as Paul treats it. I believe this can and will launch you on a journey that will lead you to experience more freedom and joy than you have known so far in your Christian life. In claiming the resources God provides, you can truly experience freedom from demonic oppression.

Each of the following five parts of this book treats a portion of Ephesians that explains a different piece of God's armor. Each part follows the same basic plan. (The final part of this book, the conclusion, will discuss the sword of the Spirit.)

In his letter to the Ephesians, the apostle Paul focused on certain schemes that Satan has hatched to try and wreck our lives. Thus, we begin each part of this book by describing a particular scheme of Satan. You will see how Satan has attempted to work in your life, and how evil spirits might have gained a foothold from which to harass and oppress you.

Next we examine a relevant piece of armor. How did it protect the Roman infantryman? And how, by analogy, does it protect you from Satan's scheme? What, for instance, does Paul teach about salvation, and how does that teaching function as a helmet to protect you against one of Satan's schemes?

Then we look in some depth at the truth Paul is revealing. Once you understand the lesson Paul is teaching and how that truth is meant to function in your life, we move on to see how you can claim it and put it into practice—right now!

The final chapter in each section is especially important. It explores ways you can respond to the truth you have learned, and by responding slam the door on any evil spirits that have attacked you or might try to attack you using that scheme. Not only will you discover how to slam the door on evil spirits that might try to attack you in the future, you will lay the foundation for expelling any that might be oppressing you now.

That is why I am so excited to share with you through this book the freeing truths I have been teaching in my Freedom Workshops. Our battle really is spiritual, as Paul wrote to the Ephesians. It is a struggle "against the rulers, against the authorities, against the powers of this dark world and against the spiritual forces of evil in the heavenly realms." This is a struggle that we need to win if we are to be all that God intends us to be. It is a struggle that we *can* win . . . if only we understand Satan's schemes, and put on the armor God provides for us.

PART 2

THE HELMET OF SALVATION

EPHESIANS 1:1–23

5

Satan's Scheme

To understand the first scheme of Satan that Paul deals with, we have to delve into personal history—history that is unveiled for us in one of David's psalms. David is meditating on his own history, but what he describes is our history, too. David praises God, saying,

> You created my inmost being;
>   you knit me together in my mother's womb.
> I praise you because I am fearfully and wonderfully made;
>   your works are wonderful,
>   I know that full well.
> My frame was not hidden from you
>   when I was made in the secret place.
> When I was woven together in the depths of the earth,
>   your eyes saw my unformed body.
> All the days ordained for me
>   were written in your book
>   before one of them came to be.
>
> Psalm 139:13–16

David sees himself as God's work; he realizes that he has been designed purposefully to be just the person that he has become.

Picture Jesus personally selecting one egg from the many David's mother produced, and holding it in His left hand. Then watch as He carefully selects one sperm from the millions produced by David's father, Jesse, and holds it in his right hand. Each contains just the genetic matter God intends to blend together to produce this unique person—David, shepherd, psalmist, king of Israel. Now, as we watch, Jesus brings His two hands together, uniting the sperm and the egg. Even more, Jesus supervises the union of the two so that just the right traits are produced as the genes find their places along the chromosomes.

Psalm 139 communicates a vital truth. David, writing under the inspiration of the Holy Spirit, has recognized himself as God's personal creation. David looks within and says, "*Your works*"—for David *is* God's work—"are wonderful, that I know full well." As a work of God, David is special, for it is the Lord who "created my inmost being."

You, Too, Are God's Work

The truth is that you, too, are God's creation. He designed you to be just the person you are. He chose the sperm and the egg; He supervised their union. Your height, your eye color, your looks, your innate gifts and talents are just what God intended. You might think that your nose is too large or wish your IQ were a few points higher, but never forget that God chose you to be you, nose and all. Through you, God will reveal something of Himself that will never be seen through anyone else.

God chose you to be you. He shaped you and He intends for you to have a fulfilling and meaningful life.

And Satan hates that.

Satan's goal is to damage and destroy you, to keep you from maturing into the person that God intends you to become. And Satan has a strategy designed to accomplish this destructive purpose: *His scheme is to block your development by convincing you that you are worthless.* Satan intends to convince you that you are flawed, weak and inadequate. His strategy is to persuade you that you are so far from "wonderfully made" that you will never step out and become all that God intends you to be. And Satan uses sins that others have committed against you to reach that goal.

Satan's Tactic

One of my students at Wheaton College was a wrestler in high school. His father was a perfectionist, always demanding more. When my student won the state wrestling championship in his weight class, his father's only comment was, "You should have pinned him sooner."

That dad sinned against his son. Imagine how the father's shameful comment hurt, and think of the lie it planted deep in his son's mind and heart. "You can never be good enough. You always fall short." When I knew this young man in college he was falling far short of his potential, and was miserable. What a contrast between that father's words and Paul's words of encouragement to the Corinthians: When Jesus returns, "each will receive his praise from God" (1 Corinthians 4:5)!

We all experience hurts that Satan can use to implant lies. One woman I know had only two birthday parties as a child, one when she was five and the other when she was ten. And at ten she had to bake her own cake. Her parents refused to celebrate her life. How do you suppose that made her feel as a child? How do you suppose it has affected her as an adult?

So many of us as children suffered verbal, physical or sexual abuse from adults. So many of us were humiliated or shamed. So many felt abandoned or responsible when parents divorced. So many were bullied or ridiculed by peers. The truth is that each one of us has been deeply wounded by the words or actions of significant others. I know you can look into your own life and find deep hurts that still make your heart ache.

Satan's strategy is to use the wounding words and actions of others to persuade us that we are not "wonderfully made" at all. Satan intends to convince us that we are flawed and useless, that our lives can never have meaning, that we deserve all the pain that we experience. Satan uses the sins others commit against us to corrupt our image of ourselves and to plant debilitating lies deep within our hearts and minds. Lies about who we are. Lies designed to make us feel weak and helpless. Lies intended to fill our lives with guilt and misery. Lies intended to rob us of the joy of knowing that we truly are wonderfully made, designed by God to be the unique individuals we are.

Stop for a moment. Remember how others have hurt you, and think of the messages that were imbedded into your heart by their words and actions.

Here is a list of some of the lies that Satan wants us to believe about ourselves.

Satan's Lies

I'm so stupid.	No one will ever love me.
People would be better off if I were dead.	I'm ugly.
I don't deserve to be happy.	There's no use trying.
I'll never amount to anything.	God can't love me.
It's always my fault.	I'm not good at anything.
I'm useless.	I'm weak, no good.
God must hate me.	I hate myself.

I might as well kill myself.	I'm a bad person.
Nobody cares.	Why should anyone care?
I'll never change.	It will never get better.
I'm going to die alone.	Nothing I do is important.
I have never done anything worthwhile.	I deserve to be miserable.

Look back over this list. Do you ever find yourself thinking some of these thoughts? Most people do at times. Some of us feel this way about ourselves almost all the time.

Normally thoughts like these, which I have labeled "Satan's Lies," can be traced back to hurts others have inflicted on us. We were ignored by our parents. We were scolded and condemned for every mistake. We were bullied at school, or laughed at and ridiculed. The chances are that if you try to recall the first time you had any of these thoughts, you will be able to trace it back to an experience in your childhood or adolescence.

But the fact is that such thoughts about ourselves are lies. Oh, the thoughts are real enough. The shame or humiliation we feel is real, too. But, nevertheless, thoughts like these are Satan's lies, planted in our minds in an effort to keep us from discovering who we truly are, and what wonderful potential we have. Satan uses the sins others commit against us to keep us from discovering that we are marvelously and wonderfully made, and that we truly are special.

6

The Helmet of Salvation

The last piece of armor the Roman legionnaire put on was his helmet. The original helmet, called a *coolus*, was like a metal skull cap made of iron covered with bronze. A decade or so before Paul wrote his letter to the Ephesians, the Roman helmet was redesigned, with a piece added to cover the back of the neck and hinged cheek-pieces added to protect the face. This helmet, called a *galea*, provided complete protection for the head.

In naming this piece of armor the "helmet of salvation," Paul uses a grammatical construction that makes one thing clear: What protects our hearts and minds from the first of Satan's schemes—his lies—is an understanding of salvation itself. But how?

In Romans 12:2, the apostle reminds us that we are to "be transformed by the renewing of your mind." The word translated "mind" is *nous*, which means "perspective." What Paul is saying in Ephesians is that our salvation provides a perspective that protects us from Satan's lies.

But what is this perspective that is reshaped by understanding salvation? As Paul goes on in Ephesians 1:3–23, it becomes increasingly clear that salvation provides a unique perspective on who we are. When we understand what God has done to provide salvation, we begin to grasp how truly significant we are and how much we are loved. We begin to see ourselves as truly special.

Satan's Goal

Satan is intent on convincing us that we are weak and helpless, nothings and nobodies. Satan wants us to view ourselves as unloved and unlovable. Satan wants us to feel guilty and ashamed. In fact, Satan expends every effort to keep us from accepting and appreciating ourselves as special.

In his book *Defeating Dark Angels*, Charles Kraft shares how he felt about himself growing up. He writes that feeling neglected by his father

> made me feel worthless and driven to achieve. These feelings grew into anger at myself and self-rejection. I didn't like my looks, my mind, my emotions, my name (Charlie). I felt I was "unlucky" and developed a terrible temper, probably rooted in my anger at myself and my situation. I even tried to run away from home, feeling that no one at home cared anyway. I wished continually that I could be someone else. I felt like Charlie Brown. "If anything goes right for me, it must be a mistake."

Even as an adult, Kraft could not accept the Bible's teaching about God's love. "I would often argue with God," he writes, "saying such things as 'If you really knew me, you wouldn't accept me like that.' I just could not accept God's opinion of me."

Even though Kraft went on to become a missionary, and later a professor at Fuller Theological Seminary and popular author, he continued for years to feel inadequate and unloved. Satan's lies had been planted deep. Like many Christians, Charles Kraft failed to grasp his true identity in Christ.

A New Identity

Before we were born, God was involved in shaping us. Satan uses wounds inflicted by others to imbed lies in our minds in an attempt to rob us of our joy in the persons God formed us to be. But as the apostle Paul describes the salvation God has provided for us, it becomes increasingly clear just how significant each of us is. Far from nothings and nobodies, we are the focus of God's love. In fact, *you are so important to God that each Person of the godhead committed Himself to provide you with your salvation!*

Let's look at some of those contributions.

7

So Great Salvation

One of Satan's most effective strategies is to mount attacks on your self-image. He uses the wounds inflicted by the words and actions of others to plant lies about who you are deep within your heart and mind. In Ephesians 1, Paul writes about the role of the Father, Son and Holy Spirit in providing you with salvation.

When we see the lengths to which God went to bring you into His family, one thing becomes clear: You are not a "nothing" or a "nobody." You are so significant that the God of the universe involved Himself totally in winning you to be His own. The God who shaped you at your birth has known and loved you from eternity. You are a child of the King, blessed, chosen and adopted into God's family. You are His, forever and ever.

In Ephesians 1:3–6, we discover that even before Creation, God the Father had you in His thoughts. From the beginning He chose you, He planned to bless you and He determined to adopt you as His child. As the apostle Paul continues writing, he also looks at the roles God the Son and God the Holy Spirit had in providing you with "so great salvation" (Hebrews 2:3, KJV).

God the Father's Contribution

- God the Father "blessed us in the heavenly realms" (Ephesians 1:3). Ephesians 6:12 points out that "the heavenly realms" are those from which "the forces of evil" launch their attacks. Blessed in those realms, we are guarded against the supernatural attacks of evil.

- God the Father blessed us "with every spiritual blessing in Christ" (1:3). Because of your relationship with Christ there is not a single spiritual blessing that you do not have. Satan's lie is: "There's no use trying." God's truth is that you have all the spiritual resources you need to achieve great things!

- God the Father "chose us in him before the creation of the world" (1:4) . Before the universe was created, God looked ahead and picked you out to be His child. Satan's lie is: "No one could ever love you." The truth is that God loved you long before you were born, and will continue to love you forever.

- God the Father chose us "to be holy and blameless in his sight" (1:4). Satan's lie is: "You'll never amount to anything." God's truth is that throughout eternity you will reflect the very holiness of God, and that even now you are becoming more and more like your loving Creator.

- God the Father has "predestined us to be adopted as his sons through Jesus Christ" (1:5). That word *predestined* means that God marked you out before the foundation of the world, and determined to bring you into His family as an adopted son. In the first century, adoption as a son was very special. Every tie to the old family was cut, and the adopted son took on the identity of the new family.

Any debt owed to the old family was canceled, and all the resources of the head of the new family became available to the adopted son. You, whether male or female, through your faith in Jesus have been adopted as one of God's own sons. Satan's lie is: "You are nothing." The truth is that you are an adopted son of the Ruler of the Universe. Satan's lie is: "You are a pitiful failure." The truth is that you are royalty, destined to rule with the Savior.

- God the Father acted "in accordance with his pleasure and will" (1:5). If you wonder why God the Father did all this for you, this phrase tells us. He blessed, chose and adopted you *simply because He wanted to*. You see, God the Father loves you. This love is not based on anything that you have done or have not done. Nor is it based on anything you will do. As amazing as it seems, you are vitally important to God *for yourself!*

God the Son's Contribution

- God the Son became a freely given gift (see 1:6). This verse highlights the words *grace, freely given* and *in the One He loves. Grace* emphasizes the fact that Jesus came even though you and I did not deserve to be saved. *Freely given* reminds us that there is nothing you or I can ever do to repay Christ for His sacrifice. And *the One He loves* is a reminder of how much it cost God to bring you into His family.

- Jesus shed His blood to redeem us (see 1:7). *Redemption* is an important theological term. It means to pay the price necessary to free someone from imminent threat or danger. Jesus' own life was the price He paid to free you from being condemned for your sins. Jesus died on the cross that you might live with Him forever.

- Jesus provided "forgiveness of sins" (1:7). Because Jesus died in your place, all your sins—past, present and future—are forgiven. God accepts your trust in Jesus in place of the righteousness none of us has.

- In Jesus, God "lavished on us" (1:8) the "riches of God's grace" (1:7). There is no end to God's favor. All the riches of God's grace are being poured out on you, now and forever. This does not mean that you will be given everything *you* want in this life. It does mean that in all that happens to you, Jesus will be there, working in each situation to bless you and those you love.

- Ultimately "all things in heaven and on earth" will be brought together in Christ (1:9–11). All of God's purposes will be fulfilled, and you will understand just where you fit into God's grand plan and purpose.

- When that happens, you will "be for the praise of his glory" (1:12). Satan's lie is: "Your life is meaningless." The truth is that throughout eternity you will glorify God. The Westminster Catechism asks, "What is the chief end of man?" The answer? "To glorify God and to enjoy him forever." This is your destiny. You will glorify God. And you will enjoy Him forever.

God the Holy Spirit's Contribution

- God the Holy Spirit "marked [you] with a seal" (1:13). The seal is the Holy Spirit Himself, who came into your life when you believed (see 1 Corinthians 12:13). In the first century, a wax seal closing a document or impressed on a product had several purposes. First, the seal denoted security. Second, the seal identified ownership. Third, the seal certified genuineness. The presence of the Holy Spirit in your life certifies that you are a genuine Christian. His presence is proof that you belong to God. And His presence assures you that you are safe in God's loving hands.

- God the Holy Spirit is "a deposit guaranteeing our inheritance until the redemption" (Ephesians 1:14). Jesus has redeemed you, paying the price to free you from the penalty of sin. The Holy Spirit is God's personal guarantee that when Jesus returns the transaction will be completed, and you will be freed from the slightest taint of sin.

To the praise of his glory (1:14). Paul repeats this phrase after the descriptions of the role of each person of the Godhead in winning your salvation (see 1:6, 12, 14). You were chosen, blessed and adopted as the Father's son. You were redeemed, forgiven and granted overflowing grace by Jesus. You were sealed and your ultimate salvation guaranteed by the Holy Spirit. And throughout eternity you will bring praise to the One who has saved you.

Paul's Summary Prayer

Paul now turns to God to pray for the Ephesians and for all Christians. First he asks God to enable us to know Him better (see 1:17). Then he asks God to open our eyes to understand the significance of this salvation that is ours. As God's own, you are now one of God's treasures, His own precious inheritance (see 1:18). What is more, God's resurrection power—that same power that raised Jesus from the dead—is now available for and to you (1:19–20). Not only did God's "mighty power" raise Jesus, but also it lifted Him to a position of total authority over the heavenly realms, "far above all rule and authority, power and dominion" (1:21). The most powerful of demonic forces must submit to Jesus.

Let me say it again. In Christ, *God's resurrection power is now available for and to you.* It is this understanding of who you are that constitutes the "helmet of salvation" that Paul urges us to put on. We are to reject all of Satan's lies. The lies that claim you are weak and impotent. The lies that claim you are unloved and unlovable. The lies that claim your life is meaningless and without purpose. The lies that claim you will never amount to anything.

Instead of believing Satan's lies we are to believe the truth and to live the truth. We are to put our confidence in the Word of God. We are to affirm our identity as God's dearly loved children, empowered and enabled by God Himself to triumph in all life's challenges.

To the praise of the glory of God's grace.

8

Putting on the Helmet of Salvation

How can you "put on" the helmet of salvation? That is, how can you change those beliefs and feelings about yourself that are rooted in Satan's lies, to find joy and freedom in affirming the person you really are in Christ?

The change normally does not happen overnight. If you have what people call a "poor self-image," Satan will go to great lengths to maintain that fiction. But as you consciously reject the lies and affirm the truth, and begin to live in the power Jesus provides, joy and freedom will come. Here are some suggestions to help you.

Speaking the Truth

Start now by reading aloud—and rereading often—the following confessions, renunciations and declarations.

Confessions

Loving Father, I confess that I have believed Satan's lies about who I am. I have accepted defeat and humiliation as though these were my due. I have failed to live as the new creation Your Word says that I am. For all this I ask Your forgiveness.

God and Father, I praise You for the gift of forgiveness won for me by Christ on the cross. I acknowledge that You have forgiven me and accepted me. I acknowledge that I am Your child and an inheritor of Your Kingdom.

Renunciations

I reject Satan's lie that I will never amount to anything. I have been given gifts by the Holy Spirit and am an important member of the Body of Christ.

I renounce the lie that I would be better off dead. I have a life to live doing the will of God that will bring glory to You, my Savior.

I renounce the lie that I am not worthy to be loved. I am loved by You, Almighty God, who knows me completely, and I am worthy to be loved by others as well.

I renounce the lie that I will always be alone. I am a member of Your family, Father, and have a host of brothers and sisters who will welcome me into community.

I confess my failure to love and to like myself, and repudiate the lie of Satan that I once believed. I am accepted in the beloved. You, Lord, see me as Your treasured possession, and it is right that I both like and love myself.

I reject the lie that nothing I do is ever good enough. You, Lord, take my efforts, no matter how feeble, and work through me by Your Spirit.

I renounce the idea that there is no use trying. I reject self-hatred and self condemnation along with false guilt. And I affirm that You, Lord Jesus, will enable me to do anything that You call me do.

I renounce fear of failure and that sense of hopelessness, which are also Satan's lies. I believe Your promise, that You give me "hope and a future" (Jeremiah 29:11).

Declarations

I declare this day that I am a dearly loved child of God through faith in Jesus Christ, for I have been adopted into God's family and provided with every spiritual blessing in the heavenly realms. As one who has been given salvation provided by the active involvement of each Person of the Trinity, I declare that I will no longer listen to Satan's lies. I will daily put on the helmet of salvation, and live as the redeemed and transformed person I truly am, to the glory of God the Father and Jesus Christ, His Son. Amen.

Strengthening Your Resolve

In addition to speaking these confessions, renunciations and declarations, follow these suggestions for putting on the helmet of salvation.

1. Read Ephesians 1 regularly, and let the truth of who you are in Christ fill your heart and mind.
2. Memorize verses like the following that affirm your true identity.

> How great is the love the Father has lavished on us, that we should be called children of God! And that is what we are!
>
> 1 John 3:1

Because we are his sons God has sent the Spirit of his Son into our hearts, so now we can rightly speak of God as our dear Father. Now we are no longer slaves, but God's own sons. And since we are his sons, everything he has belongs to us, for that is the way God planned.

Galatians 4:6–7, TLB

3. Ask the Holy Spirit to expose more of Satan's lies and reveal the truth about you. Here is how:

Find a time and place where you can be alone. Pray and ask the Holy Spirit to take complete control. Look at the list of Satan's lies on page 44 and select a thought similar to one you often have had about yourself.

Ask the Holy Spirit to take you back to an incident Satan used to implant that lie in your heart and mind. Picture the incident, and let yourself feel what you felt then.

Invite Jesus to join you in that moment of time. Ask Jesus to expose the lie and to show you who you are to Him. Then give the pain of that experience to Jesus.

Let the truth Jesus shows you replace the lie that Satan planted through that incident.

4. Remember the image from chapter 5 of Jesus standing with the sperm and the egg in His hands. Picture the moment of your own conception. Stand, and stretch out your arms, envisioning that sperm and egg in your own hands. Agree with Jesus that the person you are is valuable, and that you should have been born just as you are. Bring your hands together, as if to unite the sperm and

the egg. Then thank God for the unique person that you are and that you are becoming.

5. Tape a picture of yourself as a child on the bathroom mirror. Each time you see the picture, bless the child that you were, and remind her or him of how deeply she or he is loved by Jesus.

PART 3

THE SHIELD OF FAITH

EPHESIANS 2:1–10

9

Satan's Scheme

It was an exciting offer—a job that Preston had always wanted: marketing for a Christian organization. But it would mean moving his family from California to Wheaton, Illinois. Normally Preston and his wife, Jenny, would not have hesitated to move. But it was winter, and the Chicago area was bitterly cold. They had three young children, and after his being laid off for so long, they simply did not have the money to buy three sets of winter clothes. Preston and Jenny prayed about the offer. They believed they should accept it, but had difficulty moving forward because the nagging concern for their children would not go away. Preston and Jenny were experiencing one of Satan's most common attacks.

The apostle Paul, writing to the Ephesians, is deeply aware that evil spirits are poised to attack believers. The Ephesians' struggles—like Christians' today—are not "against flesh and blood," but against demonic beings, "against the rulers, against the authorities, against the powers . . . and against the spiritual forces of evil" (Ephesians 6:12). They needed to understand how to defend themselves.

At the end of his letter to the Ephesians, as Paul thinks back over his words recorded for us in Ephesians 2, he continues to use a particular tool to help his readers remember his teaching. Drawing on the imagery of a Roman legionnaire's armor to call each theme to mind, he now writes: "Take up the shield of faith, with which you can extinguish all the flaming arrows of the evil one" (6:16).

Flaming Arrows

One goal of Roman armies was to close on the enemy in dense, disciplined formations. No army in the ancient world could consistently defeat a Roman force with its legionnaires fighting side by side, thrusting with their short swords from behind a wall of shields. So one of the strategies used by the enemies of the Romans was to hurl "arrows" at them as they advanced.

The Romans called these weapons *plumbata*, or *belos*. We might better call them *darts* or *javelins* rather than arrows. *Plumbata* (*belos*) were short, pointed metal weapons that were hurled at an advancing enemy from a distance. The intent was that the hurled *plumbata* would disable as many legionnaires as possible and, it was hoped, break up the advancing formation.

The Roman armies had a unique defense against the hurled *plumbata*. Roman legionnaires carried an oblong shield called a *scutum*. It was shaped like a door, some two and a half feet wide by four feet long. The shield was made of glued planks of wood covered first with canvas and then with calfskin. Metal rimmed the upper and lower edges of the *scutum*, and there was an iron boss in the center of the shield as well.

When engaged in close combat with an enemy, the Roman soldier held the shield in front of him. But when an advancing legion was attacked with *plumbata*, the Romans maintained their tight ranks and lifted their shields over their heads to fashion a roof. This formation was called a *turtle*. Most of the darts hurled by the enemy simply bounced off. Any flaming arrows that stuck in the raised shields were extinguished. Because of the way the legionnaires used their shields, this strategy of the enemy was made ineffective.

What Are Satan's "Flaming Arrows"?

While Paul does not explain the kinds of demonic attacks represented by *plumbata*, their characteristics seem quite clear. The dart or javelin was a weapon hurled from a distance. This was no close, personal confrontation. The *plumbata* were not primarily weapons for killing; they were designed to incapacitate, to break up an advancing formation. The *plumbata* were simply obstacles that an advancing army had to deal with before it could close in and do battle with the enemy.

Remember the couple we met at the beginning of this chapter? Preston had dreamed of putting his talents to work in a Christian organization, but when an offer came, there was an obstacle: The job was in icy Wheaton, Illinois. He had three young children and no money to get them the winter clothes they would need if they moved. He and Jenny were anxious and uncertain. Was God calling them to Wheaton? Or did their anxiety signal that a move was not in God's will? Their concern was a very real and natural one. But their situation was typical of this scheme of Satan—the "flaming arrows" that he throws up as obstacles in every Christian's way.

Most of us have had experiences like Preston and Jenny's. We are living our lives, and suddenly we are confronted by a circumstance that makes us anxious or uncertain. What are we supposed to do?

Two months ago, Carl was recruited for a new job by a previous boss. Last week the company let the old boss go. Carl is worried. Will he be let go, too?

Erna was laid off from a well-paying job. She finally got another job running a busy office, at fifteen thousand dollars less than her old job paid. But now her co-workers are undercutting her with their employer. Erna is frustrated, depressed and angry. Should she stay?

At my seminary graduation services in Dallas, Texas, I was invited to speak representing the future pastors in my class. I was very encouraged that one of my professors had told me he was recommending me to a church in Enumclaw, Washington, that was looking for a pastor. I waited to hear from them. No call came. Finally, I was told that my wife and I with our two young children had to move out of our seminary apartment—in just one week! I went to see the professor to ask about the church. He had forgotten to make the call!

Satan takes delight in tossing just such "fiery darts" at you and me. His *plumbata* are those stressful circumstances that make us fearful, uncertain about what we should do next. Jesus described such situations in one of His parables as "trouble or persecution" (Matthew 13:21). When we face any situation that creates anxiety, doubt or uncertainty, the chances are that Satan is throwing *plumbata* at us, hoping to incapacitate us.

A Biblical Example

That happened to Abram and Sarah. After years in the Promised Land with no children, they became anxious and discouraged. Sarah urged Abram to have a child with her servant, Hagar. Filled with doubt and disappointment, Abram did as Sarah suggested. The result was Ishmael—and millennia of conflict between Arabs and Jews that continues to this day. Abraham and Sarah, panicking under pressure, failed to raise the shield that God provides for believers.

When trouble and persecution come, we need to understand the wonderful resource that will extinguish those flaming arrows. We need to take hold of—and raise up—the shield of faith.

10

The Shield of Faith

Our English Bibles call it "the shield of faith." And we wonder: Just what "faith" does Paul have in mind? Is it *the* faith—that is, the Good News that Jesus saves? Can just the fact that we are Christians shield us from Satan's "fiery dart" attacks? Or is it *our* faith, the trust that we exhibit in Jesus? And if it is our faith, how strong does our faith have to be to protect us from Satan's flaming arrows?

Or perhaps Paul is referring to something else entirely.

A New Self-Image?

In Ephesians 1, as we saw in part 2, the apostle goes to great lengths to describe the helmet of salvation that is meant to shape our self-image. When we grasp what God the Father, God the Son and God the Holy Spirit have done to provide us with salvation, we are overwhelmed with the realization that we are *not* nothings or nobodies. Each of us is special, adopted into the family of God. We are His sons and daughters now, redeemed and forgiven, blessed with every spiritual blessing, filled with the same mighty strength that raised Jesus from the dead.

Putting on the helmet of salvation, we see ourselves as God sees us, no longer victims but victors. With this vision of who we are in Christ we can shake off Satan's lies about our weakness and worthlessness and step out boldly, to live the lives God created us to live. We can see ourselves as conquerors, called to live out the victory Jesus won for us.

But then the first words we read in Ephesians 2 are these: "As for you, you were dead in your transgressions and sins" (verse 1).

What a comedown! Paul first urges us to see ourselves as chosen, loved, blessed and empowered. Then he states bluntly that we were "dead" in transgressions and sins.

And it gets worse. Paul goes on to say that we used to "live" in our sins "when you followed the ways of this world and of the ruler of the kingdom of the air [Satan], the spirit who is now at work in those who are disobedient" (2:2). Paul does not even stop there. He says: "All of us lived among them at one time, gratifying the cravings of our sinful nature and following its desires and thoughts" (2:3). In those days "we were by nature objects [children, KJV] of wrath" (2:3).

Paul encourages us in Ephesians 1 to develop a positive self-image. Put on the helmet of salvation, he says, and never let Satan deceive us with lies about how weak and pitiful we are. Then, with the very next breath, the great apostle seems intent on tearing down the image that he has built! He reminds us that we were spiritually dead, were slaves to sinful cravings, were citizens of Satan's kingdom and by nature deserved God's wrath.

God Had Other Plans

After providing this dreadful portrait of humanity Paul invites us to focus on God. We were totally lost. But God intervened!

Because of his great love for us, God, who is rich in mercy, made us alive with Christ even when we were dead in transgressions—it is by grace you have been saved. And God raised us up with Christ and seated us with him in the heavenly realms in Christ Jesus, in order that in the coming ages he might show the incomparable riches of his grace, expressed in his kindness to us in Jesus Christ.

Ephesians 2:4–7

Paul makes it very clear. We were totally, utterly helpless, wallowing comfortably in our sins. There was nothing we could do, nothing we even *wanted* to do, that would cause us to be "made alive" with Christ.

But then God acted. God gave us life in Christ. God raised us up with Christ. And because our salvation is entirely the work of God, you and I will be on display throughout eternity, living expressions of "the incomparable riches of His grace."

We are special and wonderful. But that is only because God was involved in shaping our inmost being in the womb, and only because God in Christ made us spiritually alive.

The reason Paul writes as he does in Ephesians 2 is simply because he wants us to realize that we are to depend totally on God, and not on ourselves.

This Is Not of Ourselves

As Paul goes on in Ephesians 2, he further underlines the fact that our salvation is the work of God alone. Note verses 8–10:

God Acts	We Do Not
• By grace you have been saved	—and this not from yourselves, it is the gift of God—not by works, so that no one can boast
• For we are God's workmanship	

God Acts	We Do Not
• Created in Christ Jesus	
• To do good works, which God prepared in advance for us to do	

If you are familiar with Ephesians 2:8 you will notice that I left something out. The text says, "For it is by grace you have been saved, *through faith*—and this not from yourselves, it is the gift of God."

The Greek word translated "faith" is *pisteos*. The thought underlying the *pistis* word group is that of reliability or trustworthiness. Thus, the word here can mean either "faith" or "faithfulness," depending on whether *pisteos* is ascribed to human beings or to God. If Paul is ascribing *pisteos* to human beings, then the expression *through faith* treats faith as a commodity. If I "have" faith, then salvation comes through the faith that I exercise. But if Paul is ascribing *pisteos* to God, the verse should read, "For by grace you have been saved, on account of (*dia*, through) God's faithfulness." In this case Paul is saying that salvation is rooted in the very character of God as a faithful, reliable Person.

I looked through a number of commentaries on Ephesians, but only one even mentioned the possibility that Paul might be thinking of God's faithfulness. Yet the whole passage points us to just that conclusion. What contribution did we make to our salvation? None. We were dead in our sins, contentedly following the dictates of our sin nature. Paul explicitly states that we are saved by grace, "not from yourselves" and "not by works." When it comes to salvation God does it all. And because God does it all, throughout eternity you and I will display the riches of His grace.

Why, then, in a passage that emphasizes and reemphasizes God's work, and insists that salvation is "not from yourselves" and "not of works," would Paul be thinking of *our faith* rather than God's wonderful faithfulness?

No, the shield that extinguishes Satan's flaming arrows is not the strength or the measure of your faith, your trust in the Lord. The shield is and always has been the faithfulness of God as that faithfulness is revealed in a salvation rooted in God's grace and love.

Biblical imagery confirms the idea of God as the believer's shield. This is true of the Bible's first reference to a shield, where God tells Abraham not to fear for "I am thy shield, and thy exceeding great reward" (Genesis 15:1, KJV). It is true of every other shield analogy throughout the Old Testament. As the psalmist says, "My shield is God Most High" (Psalm 7:10).

11

Where Safety Lies

Remember Preston and Jenny? After lots of prayer they decided that God was calling them to icy Wheaton. Preston took the job, which was at Scripture Press Publications. The first Sunday in Wheaton the family visited a church, and someone there noticed that the children were not dressed warmly enough. When the story came out, the members of that congregation showered the family with jackets, sweaters, snowsuits, mittens and scarves. God was faithful, and He provided Preston's family with all they needed.

Back in Dallas in my seminary days, I did not know what to do. We had to vacate our apartment, and my professor had forgotten to recommend me to the church where I had been counting on candidating.

The next day after I found out about my professor's lapse, I received an unexpected invitation to visit Scripture Press in Wheaton and to interview for a job as a curriculum editor. That job later led to a teaching position in Wheaton College's graduate school, and launched me on the writing ministry that has produced more than 250 books and study Bibles, plus curricula for every age group. I am now eighty years old, and I can say that God has been faithful every step of the way.

The Path God Has Chosen

Paul has pointed out that we make no contribution at all to our salvation. It is all God's work. It is all pure grace. We are "God's workmanship," Paul writes, "created in Christ Jesus to do good works, which God prepared in advance for us to do" (Ephesians 2:10). These are exciting words. They tell us that our lives have purpose and meaning. God has a path for us to follow, a path that He marked out ahead of time. He already knows the way through every difficulty we will face.

God was aware of the need of Preston's children for winter clothing, and that little church in Wheaton was the solution He had prepared. God knew ahead of time when I would have to vacate the seminary apartment, and He used that circumstance, with my professor's forgetfulness, to redirect my life into a teaching and writing rather than pastoral ministry. The God who saves us and has a plan for our lives is faithful.

Satan wants to force us off God's path, so he hurls his flaming arrows at us—those difficulties and troubling circumstances that cause us so much fear and anxiety. He hopes that we will panic and rush ahead of God's timing or else turn and go in the wrong direction. Yet God remains faithful. As we respond to the Spirit's promptings, every difficulty will be resolved. *The God who has saved us has prepared good works in advance for us to do.* He will guide us along the path He has chosen. We may not know what that path is just now, but God will show us when, and how, to take our next step.

Faith for Today

Paul is very aware of our human frailty. He knows how hard it is for us to trust God for today. Oh, we rely on Jesus to bring us safely to heaven. But somehow it seems more difficult to have confidence that He is here, totally involved in our lives right now. So Paul reminds us often.

He writes this to the Romans: "If, when we were God's enemies, we were reconciled to him through the death of his Son, how much more, having been reconciled, shall we be saved through his life!" (Romans 5:10).

Later Paul adds,

> For I am convinced that neither death nor life, neither angels nor demons, neither the present nor the future, nor any powers, neither height nor depth, nor anything else in all creation, will be able to separate us from the love of God that is in Christ Jesus our Lord.
>
> Romans 8:38–39

Satan and his demons can cast their fiery arrows, but there is no circumstance that can cut us off from God's love or make God's love for us ineffective.

Writing to the Corinthians, Paul comments on the difficulties everyone must face. The Greek word translated "temptation" is also translated "trouble" or "test." Taking it in this second sense, Paul encourages the Corinthians by saying,

> No [trouble] has seized you except what is common to man. And God is faithful; he will not let you be [tested] beyond what you can bear. But when you are [tested], he will also provide a way out so that you can stand up under it.
>
> 1 Corinthians 10:13

Everyone faces difficult circumstances as he or she travels through life, but through them all God remains faithful. He measures the level of stress that we can bear, and provides a way out so we can stand up to the pressure.

The Way Out

King David was shocked when word came that his son Absalom was leading a rebellion against him—and that Absalom was already advancing on Jerusalem at the head of an army. David, defended only by a troop of royal bodyguards, had no choice but to flee the city.

As David fled, he remembered. He had betrayed his God by taking Bathsheba, the wife of Uriah. Then he compounded his sin. Desperate not to be betrayed by Bathsheba's pregnancy, David ordered General Joab to give Uriah a mission where he was sure to be killed. As David fled that day he drew his cloak around him and remembered. He had failed in trying to hide his sin. In the end he had confessed it openly. But, as David relates in Psalm 3, he knew that "many are saying of me, 'God will not deliver him.'" And David had to wonder: God had forgiven him, but had his sin moved God to abandon him now?

As David pondered this, he thought back over his relationship with the Lord. David had faced so many tests, so many overwhelming difficulties. Lifting up his heart to God, David cried, "But you are a shield around me, O LORD; you bestow glory on me and lift up my head" (Psalm 3:3).

Remembering the faithfulness of God, David was filled with peace. "I lie down and sleep," he writes, ". . . because the LORD sustains me. I will not fear the tens of thousands drawn up against me on every side" (Psalm 3:5–6).

This same God is your shield. He has bestowed glory on you in choosing you, blessing you and adopting you as His own child. He will never forsake you. In His faithfulness He will extinguish every flaming arrow hurled by the Evil One. So lift high the shield of God's faithfulness. And remember that you are safe.

12

Taking Up the Shield of Faith

We have learned that the difficulties and troubles that Satan brings into our lives are like the *plumbata* hurled at advancing Roman troops. These arrows, better translated "darts" or "javelins," were intended to break up the Roman formation by disabling as many legionnaires as possible. In the same way, Satan tries to use difficult situations in our lives to hinder our advance along the path God has laid out for us.

The Romans' answer to *plumbata* was to raise their shields above their heads, to fashion what they called a "turtle." The enemy's darts bounced off harmlessly. This is the image Paul has in mind as he urges the Ephesians to "take up the shield . . . with which you can extinguish all the flaming arrows of the evil one" (Ephesians 6:16). That shield is identified in our English versions as "the shield of faith." I have suggested from Paul's argument in Ephesians 2 that the shield is not *our* faith, but God's faithfulness.

How then do we follow Paul's instructions and "take up" this shield? The same way that David did when he fled from Absalom. David focused his attention not on his troubles but on God. David remembered all that God had done for him and had been to him. David affirmed, "You are a shield around me, O LORD; you bestow glory on me and lift up my head" (Psalm 3:3). With his focus on the Lord, David's heart was at peace and he advanced confidently.

Focus on the Lord

Be prepared for Satan to create difficult circumstances in an attempt to force you off the path God has laid out for you. Here are some ways you can take up the shield of God's faithfulness.

1. God has already brought you through situations in which you felt fear and anxiety. Recall one of those situations, and write down the story of God's faithfulness to you.

My Story of God's Faithfulness

_____

_____

_____

_____

_____

_____

_____

_____

2. Share the story you have just written with one other person.

3. Get a loose-leaf notebook. Write about other times when God has been faithful. Save your stories in the notebook. The next time you find yourself anxious, read through your notebook to help you focus on God's faithfulness.
4. Invite some friends over for an evening. Ask each to tell the group about a difficult time he or she faced and how God was faithful in that situation. Conclude with a time of prayer thanking God for being a shield protecting His people.
5. Look at familiar Bible stories, such as the story of Ruth in the Old Testament. Imagine you are Ruth, and write the story of God's faithfulness as you imagine she might have written it. Do the same with other Bible men and women.
6. Memorize verses that present God as a shield. Call them to mind when difficult situations arise. Here are some familiar verses in the Psalms:

> You are a shield around me, O LORD; you bestow glory on me and lift up my head.
>
> Psalm 3:3

> The LORD is my rock, my fortress and my deliverer; my God is my rock, in whom I take refuge. He is my shield and the horn of my salvation, my stronghold.
>
> Psalm 18:2

> The LORD is my strength and my shield; my heart trusts in him, and I am helped. My heart leaps for joy and I will give thanks to him in song.
>
> Psalm 28:7

> We wait in hope for the LORD; he is our help and our shield.
>
> Psalm 33:20

The LORD God is a sun and shield; the LORD bestows favor and honor; no good thing does he withhold from those whose walk is blameless.

Psalm 84:11–12

He will cover you with his feathers, and under his wings you will find refuge; his faithfulness will be your shield and rampart.

Psalm 91:4

O house of Israel, trust in the LORD—he is their help and shield. O house of Aaron, trust in the LORD—he is their help and shield. You who fear him, trust in the LORD—he is their help and shield.

Psalm 115:9–11

PART 4

THE SANDALS
OF PEACE

EPHESIANS 2:11–4:16

13

Satan's Scheme

The book of Ephesians tells us that our struggle is "not against flesh and blood, but against the rulers, against the authorities, against the powers of this dark world and against the spiritual forces of evil in the heavenly realms" (Ephesians 6:12). As we have seen, what Paul describes here is spiritual warfare against demons.

Most Christians are not quite sure about demons. We believe they exist. But we do not know exactly what they *do*. There are stories in the four gospels that tell of Jesus casting demons out of men and women. So, if demons were cast "out," they must in some sense have been "in" those individuals.

Unfortunately, as we noted earlier, our English versions translate the Greek word *daimonizomai*—which means "demonized"—as "demon possessed." Adding that word *possessed*, which is not in any Greek text, has caused much misunderstanding. *Possessed* implies that demons can take over an individual and control him or her. Actually, that level of demonization is unusual, if it happens at all.

Nonetheless, evil spirits are active in believers' lives today, as they were active in the first century. We cannot be controlled by demons, but we can be influenced by them.

When I was a child all vehicles had running boards, flat platforms extending out just below the car doors. These served as steps for a person getting in or out of the cars. My mother did not approve, but I loved riding on the running board. Sometimes Dad would roll down the front car window, let me stand on the running board with my elbow hooked through the window, and drive off.

Riding the running board is an image that helps me understand demonization. One of Satan's minions is hitching a ride with me. It is as if a demon's elbow is through a window that opens into our lives, and he is trying to make all the trouble he can. He is reaching in, tugging on our thoughts and emotions as a person might tug on a steering wheel.

But he is not in control. The demon is not steering our lives or making our decisions for us. A demon may influence us, but we are in control. We are driving our own vehicles. That is why *demon possession* is such a confusing term. No demon can override your will and take control of your life without your permission.

The Schemes Thus Far

So what are the demons who hitch a ride with us trying to do? Let's review for a moment the schemes of Satan that we have studied thus far.

The first scheme, which we discussed in part 2, involved using the deep wounds inflicted by the sinful words and actions of others to warp and twist our self-image. Satan wants us to feel unloved, unlovable, useless and hopeless. His demons whisper Satan's lies constantly, telling us again and again that we can never change, that we will always be failures, that our lives have no meaning. We learned how to deal with that scheme by putting on the helmet of salvation.

The second scheme, which we looked at in part 3, was Satan's attempt to throw difficulties and troubles onto our paths, as the Romans' enemies threw *plumbata* at them to disrupt their advancing legions. Satan wants us to panic, and either rush ahead or turn aside from the path God has marked out for our lives. Taking up the shield of faith helps us foil that scheme.

The third scheme, the one we are examining now, is to destroy our inner peace and to distort or shatter the harmony that should exist in our relationships with others.

The "Lord of Chaos"

While God calls us to peace, Satan calls us to chaos. Satan wants us to live in a constant state of hurt, shame and hostility. Satan wants us to respond with bitterness and anger when we are wounded. Satan wants us to live on edge, constantly on guard. Satan wants us to be in turmoil, suspicious of others' motives and quick to take offense. Satan wants us to remember and to nurse every hurt. And, because all human beings sin, there are occasions galore for Satan to lead us into chaos. As he led Marti.

Marti was born into a loveless home. Her mother, an immigrant from Germany to America, married Marti's father simply to stay in the country. For the rest of her life, Marti's mother bitterly regretted her choice, and she remained indifferent toward her two children. Marti thought her father loved her, but he was so weak that Marti never sensed his support.

The indifference and rejection that Marti felt from her mother's coldness toward her warped her self-image. Satan's demons spun their lies, and Marti was filled with shame, convinced that she was unworthy of love and incapable of growth or change.

But more than Marti's self-image was damaged by this attack. Marti was also robbed of inner and interpersonal peace. As Marti grew older she became more and more bitter. Her mother had no right to treat her the way she had. Her mother had ruined her life! What chance did she have with a mother like that? The more Marti focused on the things her mother had done to her and the things her mother had left undone, the more bitter Marti became.

As an adult, with a family of her own, Marti obsessed over the wounds her mother had inflicted on her. Long after her mother died, Marti would lie awake at night, remembering incidents and mouthing the things she wished she had said.

Living in chaos, a stranger to peace and wholeness, Marti allowed shame and bitterness to overflow and make her life miserable. Although she was a Christian and wanted to follow Jesus, she could never bring herself to step up when opportunities to serve others arose. Crippled by bitterness, Marti's life was empty indeed.

Marti was right about one thing. Her mother had sinned against her, repeatedly. Each cruel word and indifferent silence inflicted another wound on the child. Young children have a need to love their parents and will excuse the most terrible of sins to preserve the fiction of love. Thus, as a young girl, Marti felt the hurt, but accepted the way her mother treated her.

But as Marti grew up and began to become bitter about the way her mother's actions had affected her, Satan's demons came in force. They shamed her. They told her she had a right to be angry. They told her she had a right to be bitter, for her mother had ruined her life.

What the demons were telling Marti was only part of the truth. Her anger was justified, for she had been sinned against. But what the demons did not tell Marti was that the anger and bitterness she felt were stealing her peace. They did not tell her that shame, anger and bitterness stifle spiritual growth. The demons did not tell her that she was nourishing what Hebrews 12:15 calls a "bitter root," a root that "grows up to cause trouble and defile many." Marti was living in chaos. And every relationship she had was affected.

No wonder Paul insists that we make sure our "feet are fitted with the readiness that comes from the gospel of peace."

14

The Sandals of Peace

In the Bible, *peace* is not just absence of strife. The Hebrew word for *peace*, *shalom*, suggests far more than a truce between warring factions. *Shalom* indicates the harmony, health and wholeness that are to mark a believer's relationship with himself, with God and with others. The richness of *shalom* infuses the New Testament concept of peace. We sense it in descriptions of the believing community. In Colossians 3:12–15, Paul shares this vision of believers living together.

As God's chosen people, holy and dearly loved, clothe yourselves with compassion, kindness, humility, gentleness and patience. Bear with each other and forgive whatever grievances you may have against one another. Forgive as the Lord forgave you. And over all these virtues put on love, which binds them all together in perfect unity. Let the peace of Christ rule in your hearts, since as members of one body you were called to peace. And be thankful.

It is a beautiful and calming picture. Oh, there are tensions. That phrase *bear with each other* really means "put up with." And the fact that there is a need for forgiveness makes it clear that people still say and do things that hurt. Yet through it all, God's people know an inner peace that enables them to be compassionate, kind and patient. And through it all, peace finds expression in the love that binds them together in perfect unity. This is the life of peace to which God calls you and me.

Peace and Sandals

Paul's armor analogy in Ephesians 6 is a mnemonic device to help us remember what he teaches in the body of the epistle. The helmet recalls his emphasis in Ephesians 1 on the work of the Father, Son and Holy Spirit in salvation, reminding us that, rather than being nothings and nobodies, we are dearly loved sons and daughters of God, blessed with every spiritual blessing. The shield recalls Paul's reminder in Ephesians 2:1–10 that salvation is a work of God from start to finish. However difficult our circumstances may be, God is faithful. He has a plan for our lives, and good works for us to accomplish.

Now Paul turns to another subject, peace, which he develops in Ephesians 2:11–4:16. The equipment he selects as his mnemonic device is a pair of the military sandals worn by Roman legionnaires. Paul reminds us that we are to advance "with your feet fitted with the readiness that comes from the gospel of peace" (6:15).

Roman soldiers were fitted with special footgear. Civilians wore soft leather shoes called *calcei*. Indoors, both sexes wore slippers, called *soleae*. Roman soldiers, however, wore heavy military sandals called *caliga*, half boot and half sandal. *Caliga* were tied on with leather thongs wrapped halfway up the shin. The sole was made of several layers of leather three-quarters of an inch thick and studded with hobnails. They were an important element of the legionnaire's equipment. Roman soldiers fought side by side in tight formations. The sturdy, hobnailed boots enabled the legionnaire to dig his feet into the ground and hold his position next to his companions.

I went out for football when I was a freshman in high school. It was several weeks before I could get football shoes equipped with cleats, so I practiced in sneakers. One day we scrimmaged against another school. It was raining, and no matter how hard I tried I could not hold my place in the offensive line. My feet kept slipping out from under me. I understand completely how impossible it would be for a Roman soldier to stand against an enemy without his hobnailed *caliga*.

Paul warns us that it is impossible for us to stand against our supernatural enemy apart from the peace represented by the *caliga*—especially as we are not expected to stand against Satan's forces alone. Like the Roman legionnaire, we must take our stand in formation with our brothers and sisters in the Lord.

Paul's image of *caliga* reminds us that we are prepared to stand against the enemy's attacks only when we are firmly grounded in the gospel of peace.

This Vital Piece of Armor

Peace in Scripture has several dimensions. There is the inner peace that Jesus knew and that He promises His followers (see John 14:27). There is the peace with God that is ours through faith in Jesus (see Romans 5:1). And there is interpersonal peace, a peace meant to mark our relationships with others. As we page through Ephesians 2:11–4:16, we realize quickly that here the "gospel of peace" is the Good News of Jesus that enables us to live at peace with one another.

What is striking is that while Paul treated salvation in 23 verses and faith (fullness) in just ten verses, the apostle devotes 48 verses to his discussion of peace. Clearly peace is vital defensive armor against the spiritual forces of evil.

Paul launches his discussion of peace by providing a test case in Ephesians 2:11–21. Jew and Gentile were hostile toward and contemptuous of each other. Yet in Christ, God united them into one Body. Using this as a test case, Paul shows how it is possible to be at peace even with those who do us harm.

Paul digresses briefly in Ephesians 3:1–13. He notes that the unity the Gospel makes possible is a "mystery," something not revealed in the Old Testament but now unveiled in Christ.

Paul returns to his theme in Ephesians 3:14–21. He argues that peace is a necessity for Christians, both personally and corporately. Only as we live together in love can we fully experience the love of Christ and be filled with "all the fullness of God."

Finally, in Ephesians 4:1–16, Paul points out the powerful results of peace. When we "keep the unity of the Spirit through the bond of peace" the spiritual gifts God has given us function, the Body of Christ is built up and we become mature, "attainting to the whole measure of the fullness of Christ."

It is no wonder that Satan is intent on sowing bitterness and strife. The last thing the devil wants Christians to experience is personal and interpersonal peace!

15

Transformation

Christianity is the story of transition from chaos to peace, from hostility to love. Once we were enemies of God. Then Christ's love for us called out our love for Him, and we were reconciled to God. The first century witnessed a similar miraculous transition. Paul describes it in Ephesians 2:14–16.

> For he himself is our peace, who has made the two one and has destroyed the barrier, the dividing wall of hostility, by abolishing in his flesh the law with its commandments and regulations. His purpose was to create in himself one new man out of the two, thus making peace, and in this one body to reconcile both of them to God through the cross, by which he put to death their hostility.

Paul is writing about Jews and Gentiles. To describe them as hostile, as Paul does, is to put the situation mildly. Jews had been persecuted by non-Jews for centuries. Their homeland was occupied by the Romans and taxed mercilessly. Jewish faith and customs were ridiculed throughout the Empire, and Jews were held in contempt. Anti-Semitic riots broke out frequently in major cities.

The Jews returned the hostility. To them all Gentiles were *goyim*, dogs, immoral worshipers of idols. Observant Jews avoided a Gentile's shadow, believing contact with it would make them ritually unclean. Filled with pride by the thought that they alone knew God's Law, a law that had been given exclusively to their chosen race, Jews felt profound contempt for non-Jews.

The mutual rejection between Jews and Gentiles caused deep wounds, and those wounds festered, generating mutual bitterness, anger and hostility.

Then Jesus came to unite the two hostile peoples into a single community, the Church—a community that was to be marked by peace and love. But how could this possibly happen?

Removing the Barrier

What set the Jews apart from all other peoples was Moses' Law. That Law, given by God on Mount Sinai, prescribed a way of life that was markedly different from the way of life of non-Jews.

By the first century, most Jews considered their descent from Abraham, along with their observance of the Law, as a guarantee of God's favor. But the Gospel challenged the notion that the Jews could claim a special relationship with God through the Law. As Paul argues in Romans, God sees Jews and Gentiles alike as sinners, and so God sent His Son to die on a cross in order that human beings, Jews and Gentiles alike, could have their sins forgiven. Rather than relate to God through the Law, Jew and Gentile are to relate to God through faith in Jesus.

With the focus now on the cross, the barrier of the Law became irrelevant. So Paul reminds the Ephesians that Christ's death abolished "the law with its commandments and regulations." The thought is that the Law could no longer create hostility between Jew and Gentile because it is now inoperative—"destroyed."

Paul's illustration establishes a simple principle. For peace to exist, the barrier to peace must be made irrelevant.

For many years, Jews related to God by observing the Law. After Jesus' death both Jew and Gentile relate to God through faith in Christ, for faith both saves and empowers believers to live a holy life. With observance of the Law no longer an issue, Jewish and Gentile believers can live together in harmony. The cross was the key to making peace. The cross removed the barrier that had caused the hostility.

But how does this help a person who has no peace because of another's sins against him or her? How does Jewish/Gentile reconciliation point the way out of the chaos caused by shame, bitterness and anger from broken relationships?

The Cross Is the Key to Peace

Paul has shown that Jesus' death on the cross renders the Law irrelevant, thus removing the cause of hostility between Jew and Gentile. This is not all that Jesus' cross means to us. The cross is God's proclamation that He forgives sin. While the cross reveals God's commitment to forgive sin, Calvary also reveals something else: *The cross demonstrates that God is totally committed to punish sin!*

Look at Romans 3:25–26:

God presented him as a sacrifice of atonement, through faith in his blood. He did this to demonstrate his justice, because in his forbearance he had left the sins committed beforehand unpunished—he did it to demonstrate his justice at the present time, so as to be just and the one who justifies those who have faith in Jesus.

How could God let "sins committed beforehand"—prior to Christ's death—go unpunished? Only because God knew that He would one day send His Son to receive the punishment those "unpunished" sins deserved!

God is a God of justice. The fact that God punished sin in Christ is proof that He will punish *all* sin. Those who trust Christ are forgiven only because Jesus took the punishment they deserve. As for the sins of the rest, those who will not look to Jesus for forgiveness will bear the punishment of their sins themselves.

Because God is committed to punishing all sins, Paul tells us, "Do not take revenge, my friends, but leave room for God's wrath, for it is written: 'It is mine to avenge; I will repay,' says the Lord" (Romans 12:19).

If only in her shame and anger Marti had understood the implications of this truth. If only she had chosen to forgive and to let God deal with her mother as He chose, Marti could have known peace. And she could have become capable of experiencing peace in all her other relationships.

I wrote earlier that Marti had a right to be angry. She did. We each have a right to be angry when someone sins against us. But we do not have a right to nurse our anger. We do not have a right to take, or even to contemplate, revenge. God is the only One who has a right to punish sin, and God is committed to punishing all sin. Because of God's commitment, the sins others commit against us have become irrelevant.

I know. It does not seem fair simply to forgive people. It makes us seem weak, and we feel ashamed to be victims who take other's blows without striking back. But remember that God is in the justice business as well as in the forgiveness business. And God has said, "It is Mine to avenge; I will repay."

Ideally forgiveness involves going to a person who has hurt us to tell her how we feel. Ideally she accepts responsibility and apologizes. Extended and received in this way, forgiveness heals relationships and restores both interpersonal and inner peace. Sometimes it is impossible to confront those who have wounded us. Sometimes when we seek reconciliation the other person is unwilling to acknowledge his fault or accept our forgiveness. Even then we can choose to forgive in our hearts.

We can go to God. We can show our wounds to Jesus and put our pain in His hands. We can surrender our right to be angry and we can choose to stop being bitter. There is no shame in transferring our cause to God's court, for God is a God of justice, and He claims the right to repay.

In its most basic form, then, to forgive is to stop holding bitterness and anger toward those responsible for harming us. It is to look to the cross of Christ, to rest our cause in God's hands . . . and to know peace.

16

Experiencing Peace

Satan has two strategies for using the sins others commit against us. When we are young he uses the sins of others to attack our self-image. As we grow older he uses the sins of others to shatter our peace and drag us into chaos. Being victimized by others arouses shame, anger and bitterness. These rob us of the inner peace promised us in the Gospel. They rob us of the unity and love that make the Christian community a family. They open windows for hitchhiking demons. How then are we to respond when others sin against us?

Inner and Interpersonal Peace

Anger itself is not sin; it is an appropriate reaction to evil. Being victimized rightly arouses anger. But nursing anger leads to bitterness, shame and inner chaos. The Bible says "'In your anger do not sin': Do not let the sun go down while you are still angry, and do not give the devil a foothold" (Ephesians 4:26–27).

How do we deal with our anger at being sinned against? We forgive the offense, no longer holding others' actions against them. We consciously and intentionally stop holding bitterness and anger toward the persons who harm us. We surrender the right to deal with their sins to the God who says, "It is Mine to avenge. I will repay."

In making this choice we free ourselves from the burden of continuing to hold the other person responsible. In fact, we Christians are called to go beyond forgiveness. Jesus calls us to love our enemies, and pray for those who persecute us (see Matthew 5:44). When we release anger and bitterness and pray for those who sin against us, we close a window through which demons might have entered.

Forgiveness is intended to lead to reconciliation as well as bless us with inner peace. Jesus spoke several times of going to a person who has sinned against us and confronting him or her with his sin (see Matthew 5:23–24; 18:15–17). The purpose of the confrontation is not to condemn or to make the person feel guilty. The purpose is to give him the opportunity to confess, and then to accept the forgiveness that restores relationship. We human beings are all sinners, and we all sin. The only way to maintain community is to be quick to confess our faults, and just as quick to forgive the faults of others.

An Important Caveat about Forgiveness

It is easy to misunderstand what forgiveness entails. First, to forgive does not require you to keep on being a victim. Forgiveness is not a license for someone to keep on harming you. A wife, for instance, who is beaten by her husband is not required to stay in a situation where she or her children are endangered. We are supposed to protect ourselves from repeated victimization. Forgiving does not mean helping a person avoid the consequences of his or her actions. In the case of criminal acts, such as child sexual abuse, forgiving does not lessen our legal or moral responsibility to report a perpetrator to the authorities.

Breaking Satan's Hold

For our feet to be shod with the readiness that comes from the gospel of peace, we need to examine our hearts and free ourselves from bitterness and anger. Here is what we can do to tie on those sandals.

1. List

In the space provided here, make a list of those you need to forgive (or those who may need to forgive you).

Those I Need to Forgive

_____

_____

_____

_____

_____

_____

_____

2. Forgive

- Look over the list of Satan's lies on page 44. Select one that often describes your feelings. Ask the Holy Spirit to take you back to an early situation in which that lie was planted by someone's sinful words or actions. Let yourself feel the hurt, shame and anger you felt then. These reactions are appropriate. Accept them.

- Ask Jesus to join you in that situation. Tell Jesus that you give Him your right to be angry and your right to pay the person back for what he or she did. Hand your emotions to Jesus, and at the same time hand Him your right to repay the person for the harm done to you.

- Choose to forgive the person who sinned against you. Tell God you leave everything in His hands, that He is free to punish or to forgive the one who harmed you as He chooses.

- Repeat this process as necessary to find freedom from any bitterness or anger you feel against any person on your list.

3. Seek Reconciliation

- Go to anyone you have forgiven. (Use wisdom: Do not put yourself in a position for further harm.) Tell him of the hurt you felt and give him the opportunity to apologize and accept your forgiveness.

- Also go to anyone you may have hurt and ask his forgiveness.

4. Pray

Begin to pray for those who have wounded you, asking God to bless them. It will change your heart. And your prayers may change their lives.

PART 5

THE BREASTPLATE OF RIGHTEOUSNESS

EPHESIANS 4:17–5:7

17

Satan's Scheme

Lee, a 37-year-old father of three, developed an addiction to pornography. He stumbled onto one of the more than three million pornography sites on the World Wide Web when surfing the Internet for relaxation after working in his home office. That first image seemed to imprint itself on his mind. He could not get rid of it, and soon found himself visiting more of the ubiquitous "adult" sites. Lee felt convicted and ashamed, but he began to save images to his hard drive and searched nightly to add to his collection.

Ceres has a sharp tongue and unusually quick wit. She is known for her cutting humor—humor that contains a little too much spite to be truly funny. If confronted she shrugs off the criticism, saying, "It was just a joke. I didn't mean any harm." Yet all in Ceres's crowd are wary of her tongue and go out of their way not to cross her.

Ken is an elder in his church. He likes to think of himself as an influential person. But Ken is one of those people who hold back in any discussion. He waits carefully to see what others think. Even if he strongly disagrees with a direction in which a conversation is moving, Ken will keep his opinion to himself. Or, more likely, he will speak out in support of whatever consensus is reached. Ken believes that his pastor has some serious weaknesses, but rather than talk with the pastor about the things that bother him, Ken comments now and then on the pastor's "weaknesses" to other church members. Ken has been known to deny his criticisms when asked about them by the pastor. Ken falls seriously short of Paul's admonition, "you must put off falsehood and speak truthfully to [your] neighbor" (Ephesians 4:25).

It is not that Lee, Ceres or Ken is a terrible sinner. Lee is physically faithful to his wife. Ceres does not set out to hurt her friends. And Ken does not cheat on his income tax. Yet each falls short of living a righteous life. Ken's addiction to pornography falls into the category of impurity. Ceres's "jokes" reveal the malice she denies feeling. And Ken's withholding of his opinion is a form of deceit. Each has cracked open the door to demonization.

The Most Deadly Door

Failure to live righteous lives is perhaps the most deadly and the most common door we open to demonic oppression. The reason is that Satan has an ally in what Ephesians 4:22 calls the "old self."

Let's recap. In Ephesians 2, the apostle pens a devastating critique of our human nature. In our native state we humans are "dead in [our] transgressions and sins" (verse 1). We follow the "ways of this world and of . . . the spirit who is now at work in those who are disobedient" (verse 2). In the eyes of society we may be acceptable enough, but even in our respectability we are "gratifying the cravings of our sinful nature and following its desires and thoughts" (verse 3). But God acted, and in His great love for us He "made us alive with Christ" (verse 5).

This theme, that the spiritually dead are given new and eternal life in Christ, is a major teaching of the New Testament. Jesus, talking with Nicodemus, portrayed it as a spiritual rebirth (see John 3), and the phrase *born again* is one of the most recognizable in Christendom.

But while the believer has, and is, a "new self" (Ephesians 4:24), the natural self with which we were born still exists. So while we have and are a new self, we still have, and are, the old self. The new self yearns for and responds to God, while the old self continues to respond to sinful cravings and desires.

We Christians are a people at war within ourselves. And in the old self that continues to crave the pleasures of sin, Satan and his demons have an ally. An intimate ally. An "inside man" who, ignorant of the implications of what he is doing, is eager to open the doors through which demons may gain access to us. Thus, for example, regarding the three individuals described above, each one has failed to master the old self, and to that extent is vulnerable to future temptations to more serious sins.

This scheme of Satan to steer us from a life of righteousness is simple, but effective. Satan directs his temptations to the old self, playing on our sinful desires and passions. Because the old self is Satan's ally, all too often we surrender to his temptations.

In the brief section of Ephesians 4:25–5:4, the apostle lists activities that are generated in the old self, and activities that are generated in the new self.

The Old Self	The New Self
Corrupted by Deceitful Desires	*Like God in Righteousness*
falsehood	speak truthfully
anger	do not let the sun go down while you are still angry
stealing	work, doing something useful
unwholesome talk	building others up

The Old Self	The New Self
Corrupted by Deceitful Desires	*Like God in Righteousness*
bitterness rage brawling slander malice	be kind and compassionate, forgiving each other
sexual immorality any kind of impurity greed	[nothing] improper
obscenity foolish talk coarse joking	thanksgiving

Paul's list is representative rather than complete. There are other lists in Scripture as well. These make it impossible for us to plead ignorance of what is righteous and what is sinful. Galatians 5 contrasts the products of the flesh (a concept that is interchangeable here with the old self) with the products of the Spirit, who produces fruit through the new self.

> The acts of the sinful nature are obvious: sexual immorality, impurity and debauchery; idolatry and witchcraft; hatred, discord, jealousy, fits of rage, selfish ambition, dissensions, factions and envy; drunkenness, orgies, and the like. I warn you, as I did before, that those who live like this will not inherit the kingdom of God. But the fruit of the Spirit is love, joy, peace, patience, kindness, goodness, faithfulness, gentleness and self-control.
>
> Galatians 5:19–23

The New Self

When Paul describes the new self, he reminds us that our new self was "created to be like God in true righteousness and holiness"

(Ephesians 4:24). That word *true* is important. It is not enough for a Christian to be a "good person" as the world or even as the church judges goodness. We are called to a higher standard.

Peter strikes the same note, writing that "just as he who called you is holy, so be holy in all you do; for it is written: 'Be holy, because I am holy'" (1 Peter 1:15).

One day Lee decided that he had to break free from his addiction to pornography. (Let me mention that the widespread nature of this addiction is a sad commentary on our culture. Students at a Christian college in the United States were asked how many of them were troubled by a pornography habit. Nearly 90 percent of the college men and 70 percent of the women admitted anonymously to pornography addiction.)

Lee tried to break his habit, but failed again and again. Finally he confessed his struggle to three men he meets with weekly for prayer. It was hard to admit his hidden addiction. His three friends prayed for him and offered him accountability. They also urged him to share his struggle with his wife. This was even harder for Lee, but he took the step and confessed what was in reality emotional unfaithfulness. With the support of his wife and friends, Lee wiped the images from his hard drive, blocked his access to pornographic sites and is now free and living a righteous life.

18

The Breastplate of Righteousness

The very name says it: This piece of armor is essential. The Roman breastplate covered the *thorax*, a Greek term indicating the chest or trunk. As such the breastplate, the *thoraka*, protected the legionnaire's vitals. A thrust to the chest might penetrate the heart—a killing blow. In Paul's time, the typical Roman soldier's breastplate was a metal plate worn over a leather garment. Soldiers who could afford it might strap the breastplate on over a coat of mail that protected both the front and the back.

The grammar of Paul's instruction here makes two things especially clear. The spiritual breastplate of the Christian is righteousness. And the aorist middle participle Paul uses indicates that the breastplate is something that an individual himself is responsible to put on

Four Types of Righteousness

The Bible has much to say about righteousness. Underlying the Hebrew word group *sadaq*, which is translated "just" as well as "righteous," is the idea of conformity to a standard. Old Testament saints were considered righteous when their personal and interpersonal behavior conformed to the moral and ethical norms established by God. This view is reflected in Deuteronomy 6:25, where Moses announces that "if we are careful to obey all this law . . . as he has commanded us, that will be to our righteousness."

Yet there was no confusion about one point. Humans might be righteous *comparatively*, as illustrated by King Saul's admission to David that "you are more righteous than I" (1 Samuel 24:17). But only God is righteous *perfectly*. Measured against the divine standard of perfection, "there is no one who does good, not even one" (Psalm 14:3). As Paul puts it, "All have sinned and fall short of the glory of God" (Romans 3:23).

Alongside comparative and perfect righteousness, the Old Testament describes a third kind of righteousness: *imputed* righteousness. Knowing that no human being could live up to the standard that God's own righteous character demands, love moved God to accept those who trust Him despite their flaws and failures. Scripture says of Abraham, "Abraham believed the LORD, and he [God] credited it to him as righteousness" (Genesis 15:6).

The significance of this stunning statement was lost on the Jews of the first century. As Paul says, in their approach to religion they "sought to establish their own" righteousness, and "did not know the righteousness that comes from God" (Romans 10:3). In contrast, the New Testament fully develops the theme of a relationship with God based on faith rather than on works. It is on the basis of our faith response to the Gospel's promise of forgiveness and eternal life in Jesus that God imputes to us a righteousness we do not have. "The words 'it was credited to him' were written not for him [Abraham] alone, but also for us, to whom God will credit righteousness—for us who believe in him who raised Jesus our Lord from the dead" (Romans 4:23–24).

This theme is so central to the New Testament that some, reading in Ephesians 6 of a breastplate of righteousness, conclude that Paul must be referring to this God-given imputed righteousness that cloaks us from the moment we believe. But they overlook a fourth kind of righteousness to which the New Testament testifies.

Jesus did not suffer simply to take us to heaven when we die. Jesus died to rescue us "from the dominion of darkness" and to bring us "into the kingdom of the Son he [God the Father] loves" (Colossians 1:13). This rescue calls for a revolution in our lifestyles. We are no longer to gratify "the cravings of our sinful nature" or to "follow its desires and thoughts" (Ephesians 2:3).

To make a godly Kingdom lifestyle possible, God gave us His Spirit. Through the promptings and the power provided by the Holy Spirit, we are now able to offer ourselves to God "as instruments of righteousness." "For," Scripture promises, "sin shall not be your master" (Romans 6:13–14). Developing this thought in Romans 8, Paul reminds us that in Christ, God condemned sin "in order that the righteous requirements of the law might be fully met in us, who do not live according to the sinful nature but according to the Spirit" (verse 4).

It is true that imputed righteousness is a dominant theme in the New Testament revelation. But God intends those to whom He credits righteousness on the basis of Jesus' cross to live righteous lives here and now. This fourth kind of righteousness is *realized* righteousness, a life lived in harmony with God's will here in this dark world, now in this present time.

Which Is the Breastplate?

So as we look at the breastplate of righteousness we need to be clear about which righteousness Paul has in mind. Is it perfect righteousness, comparative righteousness, imputed righteousness or realized righteousness? And the answer, clearly, is that Paul is speaking of realized righteousness. The breastplate that protects our vitals from the most deadly of Satan's thrusts is maintaining a good, holy and righteous lifestyle here and now.

How can we be sure? I have shown that Paul is using the armor God provides as a mnemonic device to help his readers recall what he teaches in the body of the letter. All we need to do, then, is look at that section of Ephesians that corresponds to the breastplate.

When we do look at Ephesians 4:17–5:7, there is no mistaking the righteousness Paul writes about. We Christians are called to "live a life of love," and that life is powerfully portrayed. We are given example after example of the sins that marred our old way of life, and we are given contrasting examples of actions and attitudes called for in a life of love.

Paul delineates the sins we are to avoid, and the good things we are to do. And in the passage he calls for us to "take off" the old, and to "put on" the new—a call that reminds us of that aorist middle participle I noted earlier, which indicates that we are responsible for putting on the breastplate ourselves.

We need the breastplate desperately. Realized righteousness blocks what are perhaps the most deadly and the most common avenues of demonic assault, which we discuss in the next chapter.

19

Vulnerability

I closed the last chapter by noting that righteousness blocks
the main entry points through which the most deadly and
common demonic assaults may gain access to our lives.
What are these entry points? There is general agreement among
deliverance ministers that demons enter through four primary
doors.

Demonic Entry Points

Demonization most often is associated with these four entry
points: trauma, a sinful lifestyle, the occult and the family line.

Trauma

The *American Heritage Dictionary* defines *trauma* as "an
event or situation that causes significant distress or disruption."
This is a very broad category, and events that might not bother
some can be debilitating for others. Still, this is the most common

entry point for demons. Quite often trauma experienced in childhood, due to such things as a parent's illness, divorce, abuse or simply emotional distance, seems to open the way. In such cases there is typically a negative impact on the self-image, and shame or anger creates chaos and robs us of peace. Adult traumas may have the same devastating impact.

Along with the breastplate of righteousness, the helmet of salvation, which establishes our identity in Christ, and the sandals of peace, which restore inner and interpersonal harmony, are especially important resources for those who have experienced childhood or subsequent traumas that opened the door to demonization. Also important is the shield of faithfulness. Focusing on the faithfulness of the God who protects us can reduce the anxiety that also opens the door to demonic oppression.

A Sinful Lifestyle

Sin also opens the door to demonization. This is the second most common entry point. Paul warns, for instance, against the sin of acting in anger, adding "do not give the devil a foothold" (Ephesians 4:27). Sins in this regard are usually done knowingly and habitually.

The Occult

Scripture's prohibition against any type of occult activity is especially clear. The "detestable practices" listed in Deuteronomy 18 include divination, sorcery and the interpretation of omens and witchcraft (see verses 9–12). The reason for the prohibition is that the supernatural beings reached through the occult are in fact demons.

This is the most difficult entry point to deal with, because any attempt to control or gain knowledge through the supernatural is a tacit invitation to demons to enter one's life. It provides demons with a strong legal right to be present. To expel such demons an individual must confess as sin the practice that provided access, and repudiate it completely.

Authority Figures and the Family Line

Those in authority can open the way for demonic access to those in their care—parents speaking curses over their children, for instance. In many cultures dedication of children to a pagan deity is common practice. In every culture, demons appear to associate themselves with families, so that particular sicknesses, struggles or sins travel down through the generational lines.

Living a righteous life is an essential defense against demonization. Demons are eager to see to it that the practice of any sin sprouts into a habit, blossoms into a compulsion and reaches full flower as an addiction.

Intimate Allies

Paul describes the old self as the part of us that is "corrupted by deceitful desires." That is, the things we desire may appear to be something we will enjoy, something pleasurable or satisfying. But rather than satisfy they corrode. Look at some of the things on Paul's list of the works of the old self.

- *There is falsehood.* We deceive to avoid exposure, but lies cause us to withdraw even deeper into hiding, leaving us more lonely and isolated.

- *There is sexual immorality.* We seek pleasure in sex, but in treating others as objects we become objects ourselves. In robbing others of the respect due them we surrender our self respect.

- *There is greed.* We hunger for things, and in the process
  we exalt money and possessions to the throne that rightly
  belongs to God. We end up worshiping deaf and dumb
  idols that will never meet our needs or come to our aid
  when we are in distress.

Worse still, when we turn our old self loose to pursue its
deceitful desires, we lose the mature new self God is calling
us to become. And we throw open the door to demons who
are eager to oppress us. Demons who will urge us to continue
to live empty and unsatisfying lives. Demons whose goal is to
prevent us from becoming the persons God created us to be,
and prevent us from walking in that path where we can find
fulfillment by performing the good works God has planned
beforehand for us to do.

20

Putting on the New Self

I noted earlier that in Paul's exhortation to put on the breast-plate of righteousness, the instruction is given in an aorist middle participle. That particular grammatical construction indicates that each of us is responsible to put on our own breastplate. We are responsible to choose to live righteous lives.

But the aorist middle does not mean that we are to do this alone. God has placed us in a family of brothers and sisters, and as family we are to support and encourage each other. As Lee found when facing his addiction, the support of brothers and sisters in Christ can be crucial in successfully putting off old-self issues and putting on that new self, which was "created to be like God in true righteousness and holiness."

Support Groups

One of the most important things a person seeking deliverance from any of the schemes of Satan can do is to become a member of a small support group. The particular size of the group is not critical, although I recommend groups of four to seven members. What is important is that the group be a safe place, where each person can share his or her life honestly without fear that others will gossip. It is equally important that the group be an accepting place, where each person is confident of the love, the encouragement and the prayers of other members. It is also generally best for women to meet in a women's group, and men to meet in a men's group.

When I conduct a Freedom Workshop in a local church or community, I recommend that those who want to follow up the teaching form "Live Free Support Groups." I provide lesson plans to focus the groups' sharing on issues raised in the workshop and to help them put on the full armor that God has provided to protect us from Satan's schemes.

I have included "Live Free Support Group" lesson plans as Appendix B in this book. Additional lesson plans are available on my blog, www.demondope.com. I strongly encourage you to join with others and study this book together, and when you finish to continue together for at least six weeks as a "Live Free Support Group."

Steps to Take Now

Please do not wait to take steps to put off the old self and put on the new righteous self. There are important things you can do right now. Follow the approach outlined below.

Look Inside

First, take some time for self-examination. Ask the Holy Spirit to search your heart and identify old-self issues with which you need to deal. These will generally fall into one or more of the following categories. Write down any issue the Spirit brings to mind.

Attitudes
Habitual choices
Habitual responses
Compulsive actions
Addictions

Act on What God Shows You

Deal with the issues you identified as follows:

1. Repent. Acknowledge as sin the things the Holy Spirit brings to mind. Confess to anyone you have hurt and ask his or her forgiveness. It often helps to acknowledge your issues to a friend who can affirm (announce) that you are forgiven. (See James 5:16; 1 John 1:9.)
2. Repudiate. Reject the sin and determine to do what is honoring to the Lord.
3. Relate. Tell two people close to you (one of them being your spouse if you are married) about your issue and your commitment to put off this expression of the old self. Seek their prayer support and encouragement, and report to them your successes and failures.
4. Rely. Rely on the Holy Spirit to transform your old-self attitudes, choices, responses and compulsions, and to free you from any addictions.

PART 6

THE BELT OF TRUTH

EPHESIANS 5:8–6:9

21

Satan's Scheme

We have seen how Satan plants lies in our hearts using the sins of others. His goal is to make us weak and ineffectual. Against such lies about our identity, God provides the helmet of salvation. We have been chosen and loved by the Father, redeemed and blessed by the Son, and are empowered by the Holy Spirit. Filled with wonder that we are so important that each person of the Godhead actively participated in winning us salvation, we reject Satan's lies about who we are. We are not nothings and nobodies. We are God's dearly loved children.

But Satan has another strategy rooted in lies that he uses against us. It is a strategy designed to confuse us and lead us into paths that will make our lives meaningless and empty.

Satan first used this strategy in Eden. There God warned the first pair against eating from the Tree of the Knowledge of Good and Evil. Eating its fruit, God said, would lead to death. When Satan entered the Garden in the guise of a serpent, he set out to wean Eve from the truth with lies. Satan told Eve that rather than leading to death, eating the fruit of the forbidden tree would lift her to become like God. God, Satan said, was jealous, and did not want humans to possess what the fruit offered.

Eve listened to the lies and then relied on her senses. The fruit looked and smelled good. And she wanted what Satan promised. So Eve chose to believe Satan's lie rather than God's truth. Eve was deceived; Satan's lie had snared her.

Note the difference between Satan's attack on our self-image and this ploy. Here Satan presented a new way to look at the forbidden tree, a different way to see it. In response Eve abandoned God's revelation, bought Satan's distortion and ate.

In a confrontation with the Jewish religious leaders, recorded in John 8:44, Jesus brought both Satan's character and one of his strategies into clear focus. Christ said, "When he [Satan] lies, he speaks his native language, for he is a liar and the father of lies."

The Bible has much to say on this strategy of Satan. In His Word, God has revealed what is right and good and ultimately leads to blessing. Satan's strategy is to use lies to confuse humankind, to entice us to choose something that may seem desirable but which, in fact, is illusory and will ultimately lead to sorrow and regret. Among the more than half dozen Hebrew and Greek terms that unveil this strategy are words translated "illusion," "deception," "to deceive," "to be deluded," "to make a fool of," "deceitfulness," "delusion," "empty," "worthless" and "fantasy."

While God reveals beliefs, attitudes, values and a way of life that bring blessing, Satan spins lies that appeal to "the cravings of sinful man, the lust of his eyes and the boasting of what he has and does" (1 John 2:16). Such attitudes and values are woven into what Scripture calls the *kosmos*, the "world," which we might better render here as "human culture." Of our cultures, the apostle John notes that "the whole world is under the control of the evil one" (1 John 5:19).

Our society, like every human society, has chosen to believe and to act on Satan's fantasies rather than on what God has revealed. We all live among people who, like Eve, have chosen to believe Satan's lies. The world values possessions more than persons, achievement more than relationships. The world believes that a bigger house or a newer car will bring happiness. The world is attracted to beauty rather than character, and the world celebrates "success" while ignoring family.

Satan has spun a web of lies about what is important in life, about what we should value, about what will make our lives significant and meaningful. In this world of illusions under the control of the evil one, we desperately need the belt of truth, a defense against the lies woven throughout every society by Satan.

22

The Belt of Truth

The *New International Version* translation of Ephesians 6:14 reads: "Stand firm then, with the belt of truth buckled around your waist." It is a vivid translation. We can imagine the Roman legionnaire, strapping on a wide belt. We can almost see the sword and perhaps a knife hanging from it.

The only problem is, the image the translation conjures up is about as wrong as possible! First of all, this "belt" was not the last thing the Roman infantryman put on when equipping himself for battle; it was the first thing he put on.

And second, even if we imagine a soldier strapping on his wide belt first, he simply cannot kneel to wrap sandal straps around his calf with a sword in the way, or put his breastplate and mail shirt on over his sword belt. So what does it mean?

The Greek says literally, "Stand, having girded your loins with truth." It does not mention a belt, or define exactly what equipment it was that the Roman soldier girded around his loins. While "girding one's loins" is a common expression in

Scripture, it generally describes a Jewish man pulling his long garment through his legs and tucking it around his waist for greater freedom of motion as he worked. Ephesians 6:14 is the only verse in Old or New Testaments that mentions girding in a military context.

Vital Support

My wife, Sue, is dedicated to taking care of me. And it is a big job. One of the things she insists on is that I do not do any heavy lifting. Even if I have to lift something relatively light, she wants me to put on a girdle-like support with straps that loop over my shoulders and a band held by Velcro around my waist from ribs to hip. Even though I sputter a bit, I know it helps. I can feel it supporting and strengthening my core, just as weight lifters use thick leather belts to strengthen their core when they hoist hundreds of pounds.

What the Roman legionnaire girded himself with was a sturdy, tightly wrapped leather girdle that reached from ribs to loins. Cinched tightly, the girdle provided essential support to his core. The Roman legionnaire, standing with fellow soldiers in tight formation against barbarians who threw themselves against the Roman lines, needed all the core support he could get!

It should be no surprise that Paul says, "Stand firm then, with your loins girded with truth." We need all the core support we can get if we are to stand firm against the spiritual forces of evil.

Living by God's Word, wrapping God's truth tightly around us, provides just the support you and I need. After all, this is what Jesus taught in John 8 when He told His early followers that if they put His words into practice they would know the truth, and the truth would set them free.

The First Step

Being girded with truth is the first step in putting on God's armor, for truth is key to wearing the rest.

> The helmet of salvation protects us only as we live out our true identity in Christ.
>
> The shield of faith enables us to advance despite adverse circumstances only as we rely on the trustworthiness of the God revealed in Scripture.
>
> We strap on the sandals that bring inner and interpersonal peace only as we commit our cause to the justice of God and forgive those who sin against us.
>
> The breastplate of righteousness wards off the devil's thrusts only as we identify and reject sin in order to live godly lives.

Fully equipped by living out the truths God shows us in Scripture, we can and will stand against all of Satan's attacks.

23

Illumination

Kipling spins the tale of David Balfour in his book *Kidnapped*. As the story opens, David's father has died, and an attorney sends David to his uncle to claim his inheritance. Night is falling as David approaches the crumbling castle where his uncle lives. The specter of the aging ruins in the growing dusk sends a chill through David, but the boy has nowhere else to go. Hesitantly he approaches the massive oaken doors set into ancient stones. He knocks. He waits, and then knocks again. Finally, frightened by the sudden darkness that has fallen around him, he pounds on the doors desperately.

As last he hears shuffling steps, and a smaller door that David had not noticed opens. In the light of a single candle, David sees the face of a stooped old man who peers with hostility out into the darkness. "It's David, your nephew."

The old man brings David inside and leads him through icy, empty hallways into a barren kitchen. The uncle sits down at a decrepit table where he is eating a bowl of gruel. Despite the chill there is no fire burning in the grate, and when David offers to build one the old man shakes his head. Coal is expensive, and the old man will not spend an extra farthing to warm the room.

David tells the story of his father's death and hands his uncle the will and the letter prepared by the attorney. The uncle puts it aside. They will speak of it in the morning. Now it is time for bed. The uncle points to a flight of stone steps leading up into even deeper darkness. David is to climb the steps until he comes to an open doorway. Inside he will find a bed where he is to spend the night. When David asks for a candle to light the way, his uncle refuses. He will waste no money on extra candles. He instructs David to feel his way by keeping one hand on the wall until he comes to the doorway that leads into his room.

David protests, but his uncle insists. So, hesitantly, David begins making his way up the stairs. The darkness is so deep that David cannot even see the great stones set in the castle wall. With one hand pressed against those chill slabs, David stumbles up the rough stone steps until he reaches what seems to be a landing. With arms outstretched David is about to step into what he has been told is his room.

Suddenly there is a flash of lightning, and David sees that the stairway ends in nothingness! Looking down David sees rocky crags on which his uncle expected him to fall to his death. The lightning flash revealed what was really there. The light showed David the truth.

Why Paul's Focus on "Light"?

As we continue reading Paul's letter, beginning at Ephesians 5:8, we are struck by two things. First, in this section regarding the belt of truth, Paul continues his discussion of a Christian lifestyle. This is the theme he emphasized in the preceding section—a section that corresponds to the "breastplate of righteousness." Second, Paul's immediate emphasis seems to be on light, not on truth.

> Live as children of light, (for the fruit of the light consists in all goodness, righteousness and truth).
>
> Ephesians 5:8–9

> Everything exposed by the light becomes visible, for it is light that makes everything visible.
>
> Ephesians 5:13–14

While Paul notes that the fruit of light is a cluster of virtues made up of goodness, righteousness and truth, we still do not understand why Paul writes as he does, or how his emphasis on light relates to the belt of truth. But there is an answer, and the story of David Balfour helps us understand.

What is the link between truth and light? Truth refers us to reality, to seeing things as they really are, to things as God knows them.

Our problem is that we human beings have lost touch with reality. We live in a world of illusions spun by Satan that appeal to our old nature, the "old man" that Paul implores us to take off. Stumbling along in this world of illusion we are unable to distinguish between right and wrong, between what will benefit us and what will harm us. We desperately need a trustworthy source of light that will reveal reality.

God has given us that beacon. It is His Word. In fact, Scripture serves as both light and truth. God's Word is true because its teachings are in harmony with reality. And God's Word is light because it makes that reality clear to us. In the words of the apostle Paul, "It is light that makes everything visible" (Ephesians 5:13).

The Meaning of "Truth"

In writing *The New International Encyclopedia of Bible Words* (Zondervan, 1999), I explored the meanings of Hebrew and Greek terms as they are used in the Old and New Testaments. The Hebrew term *'emet* and the Greek term *aletheia*, both translated "truth," indicate that which is authentic, reliable and trustworthy. God's Word is represented as truth, because it is a reliable and trustworthy revelation of reality as God alone knows it.

This underlying concept, that truth is and must be in harmony with reality, plays a significant role in the epistles of both Paul and John. In the *Encyclopedia* I wrote:

> Paul's conviction is that God has cleared away humanity's illusory beliefs and notions, and in the gospel has provided a clear perspective on reality. Through revelation we at last have reliable knowledge about God, about ourselves, about the nature of the universe, and most importantly about how to live in intimate relationship with the Lord.

p. 602

The article continues:

> The truth is not only reality as God has revealed it. The truth is reality as believers are able to experience it by making choices guided by God's reliable Word.

p. 603

Jesus: The Light and the Truth

Jesus made a number of claims that upset the religious leaders of His time. One day He announced, "I am the light of the world. Whoever follows me will never walk in darkness, but will have the light of life" (John 8:12). This was too much for the Pharisees, and they challenged Him.

The challenge quickly deteriorated into charges and countercharges, and, as we read this passage in the gospels, we sense that Jesus' opponents were not really listening to what He said. Finally Jesus shrugged His shoulders and gave up, saying. "When you have lifted up the Son of Man, then you will know that I am the one I claim to be" (verse 28).

Jesus then turned to the Jews who did believe in Him and made them a promise. "If you hold to my teaching, you are really my disciples. Then you will know the truth, and the truth will set you free" (verses 31–32). The *King James Version* puts it a little more clearly. "If ye continue in my word"—that is, if you live by what I say, if you put what I teach into practice, then you are My disciples. Then *and only then*—"ye shall know the truth, and the truth shall make you free."

Today the phrase *You will know the truth and the truth will set you free* appears on the masthead of a once-great newspaper, where it is totally misapplied. Jesus never taught that accurate information sets anyone free. He did say, however, that if we put His teaching into practice, *we will experience the truth*, and that experience of truth will free us. In living a life illuminated by God's Word, we enter the realm of truth.

Living according to God's trustworthy Word saves us from the illusions that threaten our paths. In Jesus' teachings and the words of Scripture, we are given hope. As we put our trust in that Word and live according to it, we experience what life can and should be for us.

The truth is not just something we access mentally. The truth is what life in Christ is all about. We are not called simply to believe the truth. We are called to live the truth.

It is in coming to experience truth as a lived reality that we are set free.

24

Putting Truth into Practice

It is not really surprising that the belt of truth represents putting God's Word into practice. What is surprising is what the apostle goes on to talk about after laying this groundwork. For what Paul does next is to lay out something called a "household code."

Household codes had long been popular in Hellenistic culture and there were many in contemporary secular literature. In fact, there are several more household codes in the New Testament. These codes specified the duties and responsibilities of everyone in the household. We will explore how the Christian codes differ from secular codes in a moment. But now we need to ask why Paul includes a household code here.

I believe the answer is simple. The core of any person's life is to be found in those primary relationships that exist in the family. The persons who know us most intimately, and whose lives we affect most deeply, are spouses, children and other family members. If we are to protect ourselves from Satan's schemes and the demons who carry them out, we need to be sure we are living out God's Word at home. At home, where everything we say and do has the potential to build those we love up or to tear them down. Be girded with truth everywhere you go. But be absolutely positive that you are girded with truth at home!

Household Codes

After introductory verses on the theme of Scripture as light and truth, Paul turns his attention to relationships within the family. He has exhorted us to be wise and understand what the will of the Lord is. Now he discusses God's will for spouses, children and the extended family. Living the truth is particularly important in this setting, for family relationships are the most influential in shaping an individual's personality, especially as a child but also as an adult.

Household codes were a recognized literary genre in the ancient world. Many a writer devoted treatises to household management, dispensing advice to those who made up a family unit. A surprising number of New Testament passages are of this type, discussing life in the household (see Ephesians 5:22–6:9; Colossians 3:18–4:1; 1 Timothy 2:8–15; 6:1–10; Titus 2:1–15; 1 Peter 2:18–3:7).

There is, however, a significant difference between the biblical codes and the secular. The secular codes reflect the pagan assumption that the husband/father is the absolute head of the household. These codes discuss in detail what wives, children and slaves owe to him. But they fail to mention any duties the head of the household might owe to his wife, children and slaves.

The biblical codes are radical in that the Christian husband is held accountable for loving his wife, nurturing his children without "exasperating" (provoking) them and treating his slaves with respect. The Christian husband/ father is not a dictator, but rather is God's servant, charged with tending to the welfare of all the members of his household. Whatever a wife, child or servant might owe the husband/father, he owes them even more. And Ephesians 5:21, which bridges the prior paragraph and the paragraph dealing with husbands and wives, establishes the framework for marriage and family life. "Submit to one another," Paul says, "out of reverence for Christ."

Husbands and Wives

Books have been written and churches have split over just what it means for wives to "submit" to their husbands, and for husbands to love their wives "as Christ loved the Church." Generally the debates generate more heat than light. Yet the tone of this passage is abundantly clear. Husbands and wives are to care deeply for each other. Each is to have concern for the personal and spiritual growth of the other, and they are to approach their marriage as a partnership in the deepest sense of that word. Within the context of marriage the two become one.

I did not realize it growing up, but my dad was a benevolent dictator. He truly loved my mother, and worked hard all his life to provide for her. She in turn loved him deeply. They had no major disagreements on finances, child rearing or faith, although my mother was more spiritual than my dad. They agreed that contributing 10 percent of our meager income was the right thing to do, and Dad served as an elder in our church.

But in many little ways, both of them treated Dad's needs as more important than Mom's. Dad would have accompanied Mom to Wednesday prayer meetings, as she wanted, but Wednesday was lodge night, and Dad was deeply invested in his lodge. Vacations were fishing trips, even though cooking meals and cleaning a cabin was not exactly a vacation for Mom. Growing up I was completely unaware of these dynamics. Our home was filled with love and acceptance. And I never noticed that my mother was hurting.

In my own marriage I adopted the pattern set by Dad. I love my wife and have always worked to provide for her. In the early years of our marriage I thought nothing of getting Sue whatever she felt she needed. But in my benevolence, I never noticed that there was time for us to go fishing, but no time to go the Strawberry Festival in Zephyrhills that she wanted to attend. I ignored many other things she expressed a desire to see or to do.

It was easy for Satan's demons to play on her sense of having no real influence, and cause her hurt to grow into contempt. It was easy for me to assume that I knew best—and it took me a long while to come to my senses and realize that I was failing to love my wife as Christ loves the Church.

This is the kind of thing the Ephesians household code deals with. Only as each of us takes on the mantle of servanthood and submits to others will we live out God's truth within our families.

Living the Example

I have come to realize how right the apostle Paul was to emphasize the importance of girding on that belt of truth in the home. The fact is, the family is the primary setting in which we are to wear the armor of God, and we need to help each other put it on daily.

Look at the ways in which the belt of truth affects each of the other pieces of armor we have studied thus far.

- The success of Satan's scheme to undermine a person's self-confidence relies in large part on harsh words and actions by parents when a child is young. Family members can help each other don *the helmet of salvation* by affirming each one's importance to the family and to the Lord, and by affirming the gifts given to him or her.

- The success of Satan's scheme to weaken us through anxiety is advanced as we fail to display confidence in *the shield of God's faithfulness* when a family member faces a difficult circumstance.

- The success of Satan's scheme to rob us of our ability to walk in *the sandals of inner and interpersonal peace* and create chaos depends in large part on our failure to extend and accept forgiveness quickly within the home, and to model forgiveness in our relationships with others.

- The success of Satan's scheme to entangle us in sins is far more likely if parents are not committed to putting on *the breastplate of righteousness* or fail to communicate God's standards to their children in positive, loving ways.

When I taught classes on youth ministry at Wheaton College Graduate School, I conducted a study of eighth graders at a local Christian school. My goal was to identify young people to whom God seemed very real, and to find out whether any factors in their home lives made a critical difference.

I learned that a number of factors at home had no particular impact. These included the parents' approach to discipline, whether or not there were family devotional times and the number of church meetings the family attended. But one thing made a critical difference, and allowed me to distinguish clearly between youth to whom God was real and those to whom He did not seem real. That one thing was this: If a child saw that God was real to Mom and Dad, the Lord was also real to him or her. How vital, then, that we gird ourselves with truth! How vital that we understand that God is calling us to experience the reality of Scripture every day! As the apostle Paul reminds us,

Be very careful, then, how you live—not as unwise but as wise, making the most of every opportunity, because the days are evil. Therefore do not be foolish, but understand what the Lord's will is.

Ephesians 5:15–17

PART 7

CONCLUSION

EPHESIANS 6:10–20

25

Biblical Demonology

Ephesians 6:17–18 adds two important lessons to our goal of defending ourselves from the schemes of Satan. The text says to take "the sword of the Spirit, which is the word of God. And pray in the Spirit on all occasions with all kinds of prayers and requests."

We can understand quite easily Paul's emphasis on prayer. Our safety depends on God's mighty power. We must rely on Him and look to Him at all times, expressing all our needs and concerns. But there is something unusual about Paul's reference to the sword.

For the first time in his listing of pieces of armor, the apostle clarifies one of his metaphors. "Take the sword of the Spirit," he says, and then he reveals that the sword of the Spirit is "the Word of God." Why an explanation of the sword when there is no parallel explanation of any other piece of equipment? The reason is that each piece of armor has already been thoroughly discussed in his letter. By reading this far we already know what the helmet, shield, sandals, breastplate and belt represent.

Also note that the pieces of armor Paul focuses on throughout his book are defensive. Ephesians is about equipping believers to defend ourselves against the strategies demons use to oppress us. The sword, by contrast, is an offensive weapon.

We gather from this emphasis on defensive weaponry that it was not Paul's primary purpose in this letter to go into the question of how to attack demons. It is likely that this was something the Ephesians already understood, for they had witnessed Paul casting out evil spirits (see Acts 19:11–12). Indeed, Paul's authority over evil spirits was a major factor in the conversion of many in Ephesus and in their repudiation of magic and sorcery (see Acts 19:14–20). Certainly, too, the writings of the earliest Church fathers treat casting out demons by believers as a commonplace occurrence.

In light of the evidence of Scripture and Paul's own serious attention to demons, then, we simply cannot afford to ignore them. Demons are committed to trapping humans in as much pain and suffering as possible. We have addressed this topic of demonology to some degree thus far in this book, but in this chapter and the next (see also the appendixes), we deal with it more specifically, and to do so, we take up the sword of the Spirit, which is the Word of God.

Biblical Background

All cultures reflect a belief in evil spirits. These are explained in various ways: as spirits of the dead, as frightening supernatural animals, as gods or goddesses, or as demons. Likewise, every culture seems aware of supernatural entities that can and do harm humans.

The Bible confirms the reality of evil spirits, and offers a unique explanation. Demons were originally angels, fashioned by the Creator. But a number of the angels, led by a powerful angel named Lucifer, rebelled against the Creator. In the rebellion Lucifer became Satan, and the angels who joined his revolt became demons. Like angels, demons do not reproduce or die. Through the ages they have remained the enemies of God and, since God loves human beings, demons are also the enemies of humankind.

While the Bible does not provide a thorough explanation of the activities of demons, there are clues as to how they go about opposing God's purposes and oppressing human beings.

Demons in the Old Testament

The Old Testament says little directly about demons, but it does make reference to three major activities of evil spirits. The first is found in Deuteronomy 31:16–17, which speaks of making offerings to demons disguised as pagan deities (see also 1 Corinthians 10:18–20). False religion is energized by demons, and any supernatural accomplishment of pagan gods is the work of evil spirits.

The second is found in Deuteronomy 18:9–13, which bans all forms of the occult. The only supernatural contact made by those who practice witchcraft, sorcery, divination, spiritism, etc. is with demons. A person may gain temporal benefits from the worship of false gods or through occult means, but the demons behind these phenomena are intent on keeping humans from knowing the one true God, to their ultimate destruction.

The third insight into the activities of demons is found in Daniel 10, where a powerful demon called the prince of Persia is mentioned. The passage suggests that just as God assigned the angel Michael to look out for the interests of Israel, so Satan assigns demons to tend to his interests in the activities of nations.

Demons in the Gospels and Acts

The four gospels portray the impact of demons on individuals. Again and again Jesus meets demonized individuals who suffer from serious disabilities, ranging from chronic back pain to mental illness. In each case Jesus heals the individual by casting out the demon or demons. There is no suggestion in the gospels that all illness is demonic in origin, as many reports of healings make no reference to demons. But it is clear from this era of intensified demonic activity, as Satan marshals his forces to oppose the Son of God, that physical and mental illness may be caused or exacerbated by demons.

Jesus Himself not only casts out demons, but also gives that authority to His followers (see Luke 9:1–2). After Jesus returns to heaven, His followers, including the apostle Paul, exercise this authority. And the early Church fathers mention casting out demons as a continuing phenomenon.

Incidents recorded in the book of Acts, such as Paul's casting a demon out of a slave girl in Philippi who was telling fortunes (see Acts 16:16), suggest that some paranormal activities may be demonic in origin.

Demons in the Epistles

The epistles affirm that Satan and his demons are actively engaged in a war against humanity, but especially against believers. This war seems to be carried out on two fronts.

The first of Satan's efforts is directed at the control of culture. John tells us that "the whole world is under the control of the evil one" (1 John 5:19). In this context the word translated "world" is *kosmos*. In its theological use, as here, *kosmos* refers to the structure of society: the ways in which a society incorporates and reflects values, attitudes and beliefs. John describes human culture as *kosmos* in this way:

> Do not love the world or anything in the world. If anyone loves the world, the love of the Father is not in him. For everything in the world—the cravings of sinful man, the lust of his eyes and the boasting of what he has and does—comes not from the Father but from the world.
>
> 1 John 2:15–16

Basically, Satan influences cultures so that they appeal to humankind's sinfulness. By shaping a culture's values in this way, Satan directs human aspirations and efforts away from God and toward the temporal and meaningless. As John says, "The world and its desires pass away, but the man who does the will of God lives forever" (1 John 2:17). By influencing culture, Satan and his demons hold sway over the majority of humankind without being required to influence individuals one by one.

At the same time, the epistles make it very clear that demons pay attention to individuals, and especially to believers. We have explored Paul's directive to the Ephesians to

> take your stand against the devil's schemes. For our struggle is not against flesh and blood, but against the rulers, against the authorities, against the powers of this dark world and against the spiritual forces of evil in the heavenly realms.
>
> Ephesians 6:11–12

As we have noted, the terms *rulers*, *authorities* and *powers* were applied in the first century to the supernatural entities we know as demons. According to Paul, these entities operate "schemes" the devil has devised.

As we look through the New Testament epistles we find a number of these schemes mentioned. Demons gain a hold on believers through bitterness and anger (see Ephesians 4:26–27) and through failure to forgive (2 Corinthians 2:10–11). Those who are addicted to sin are in great danger of demonic op- pression (see Ephesians 5:3–5). Demons use the traumas we experience to block our awareness of who we are in Christ (see Ephesians 1). Demons blind us to God's revelation (see 2 Corin- thians 4:4). In these and many other ways demons seek to gain a hold on believers, on churches and on Christian ministries in order to prevent a close walk with Jesus and to block fulfillment of God's purposes in our lives.

There is considerable teaching on evil spirits in the Bible, alerting Christians to the reality of demons, the dangers demons pose and the resources God has provided to enable us to stand against "the spiritual forces of evil in the heavenly realms." In addition, we are authorized to cast them out.

26

Casting Out Demons

Casting out demons does not depend on special gifting or even special holiness. Any Christian living in fellowship with Christ can command demons in Jesus' name, and they will obey him. Many Christians today have deliverance ministries, in which they regularly cast demons out of believers.

An effective deliverance ministry, however, involves more than expelling demons. An effective deliverance ministry involves dealing with trauma, with unwillingness to forgive and with the sins and addictions that opened the door to demonic presence in the first place. Deliverance ministry is first of all about healing, and then about expelling demons and closing doors to any future demonic oppression.

This is why the apostle Paul penned his letter to the Ephesians. Once they had dealt with issues of trauma, sin, unforgiveness, etc., they needed to learn to close the door against demons by protecting themselves from the evil schemes the devil devises.

Freedom Workshop

My Freedom Workshop, which is based on the book of Ephesians, is designed to help believers deal with these same schemes of the devil that Paul addresses in teaching us about the full armor of God. Some who attend take dramatic steps toward freedom from self-rejection, anxiety and bitterness during the sessions. Others go home with resources they can use to work on these issues. Some become members of a "Live Free Support Group" and find healing there. Still others may work on issues with a Christian counselor. As healing takes place—suddenly or gradually—the grip of any demons present is weakened and they are easily removed.

During my workshops, I command any demons whose grip has been weakened by their hosts' response to the Word of God to leave those persons and not return. Whenever a church provides prayer warriors to pray with individuals after a workshop, I encourage them to command any demons to leave the persons they are praying with. And, if you are reading this book and have dealt with issues of your own, I strongly suggest you order any demons out of your own life.

Demons seem to cling to those things in our lives that we have explored in this book. They cling to the lies we believe about who we are. They cling to our bitterness and anger. They cling to our anxiety and worry. They cling to our sins and addictions. Many in deliverance ministry call such issues *legal ground*, those things that demons claim give them a right to be in a person's life. When we deal with the pertinent issues, we strip demons of their right to be present, and they respond quickly when they are commanded in Jesus' name to leave. What might such a command be like?

In the name of Jesus Christ, God the Son, my Savior, and with the authority He has given me as a child of God, I command any demons present to leave, now. You are to report to Jesus, who will do with you whatever He chooses, and you are never to return or to trouble me or any loved one of mine again.

Please turn to Appendix B for a more comprehensive study of the Freedom Workshop.

Finally, Be Strong

After helping us understand the importance of identity, trust, forgiveness, righteousness and truth—along with wielding the Word of God like a sword and remaining constant in prayer—Paul sums up the teaching of his letter with an exhortation: "Finally, be strong in the Lord and in his mighty power" (Ephesians 6:10).

The apostle is well aware that evil entities, which the Ephesians knew as the rulers, authorities and powers of this dark world, would continue to mount attacks against the young Christians. Those same entities, which we today call demons, mount the same kinds of attacks against you and me.

But in his letter, the apostle unveils the armor that God provides to protect us from the devil's schemes. And so, our core "belted" and strengthened by living the truth, the breastplate of righteousness in place, our feet fitted with the readiness that comes from the gospel of peace, wearing the helmet of salvation and shielded by God's faithfulness, we can stand against the powers of evil.

May you so stand, strong in the Lord and in His mighty power.

Appendix A

Christian Counseling and Evil

One of the most serious problems in much of so-called Christian counseling, as well as in openly secular approaches, is a far too casual dismissal of the concepts of sin and evil. These admittedly theological concepts find a chilly reception in contemporary counseling theory. Like all theological concepts, the ideas of sin and evil convey a distinctive view of reality. And counseling theories necessarily are rooted in and embody distinctive views of reality.

When the ideas of sin and evil are dismissed, however, both a counselor's diagnosis and treatment will be affected. A counselor, for example, who views sexual experimentation in adolescence as a developmental phenomenon, and rules out the notion that it might be viewed and treated as sin, will not recognize either the damage done to the individual or the healing power of forgiveness. So in this study I intend to explore the theological concepts of sin and evil, their impact on people and how persons might be counseled.

As I write from a conservative Christian perspective, any theological concept discussed here expresses the view of reality found in the Old and New Testament Scriptures.

The Concept of Evil

The study of *evil* from my research in the *New International Encyclopedia of Bible Words* is helpful here. The concept of evil is expressed in the Old Testament in the Hebrew root *ra'*. Words constructed on this root, used for describing evil actions, are variously translated "evil," "to do evil," "to be evil," "to act wickedly," "to do harm," etc. In the *Encyclopedia*, we read that

> these words are used throughout the Old Testament. They focus on two aspects of evil. Morally, they identify actions that violate God's intentions for human beings. The words are also used to describe the consequences of doing evil; the tragedy, distress, and the physical and emotional harm that come as a result of wrong moral choices. These, like the choices themselves, are labeled evil.

> p. 252

As is the case with biblical terms for *sin*, there is no room here for relativism. God presents Himself as the standard by which good and evil are to be measured, and, thus, wrong actions are often described as doing evil "in the eyes of the Lord" (see Deuteronomy 4:25, for instance). There is no hint here of the philosopher's notion of evil as an absence of good, or a representation of the gap between Creator and creature. A person is considered evil because he performs evil actions that do harm to other human beings.

But note that the same root also expresses the impact of evil acts. Thus, *evil* is not only the action, but also the result—the human "misery," "distress," "troubles," disasters," etc. that follow evil actions.

These aspects of evil as the action and the outcome are somewhat disguised in modern translations such as the *New International Version* and the *New American Standard Bible*. There the translators have chosen to render *ra'* terms by outcomes such as "harm," "disaster," "distress," "troubles," etc. This is unfortunate, as the Hebrew text clearly links evil deeds and the evils that flow from them. As stated in the *Encyclopedia*,

> We cannot really understand the Bible's view of evil until we sense the extent of the personal tragedy—the physical and psychological disaster—that results from abandoning God's way.
>
> p. 253

The Relation to Sin

There are three basic terms for *sin* in the Old Testament. Each of the three, again quoting the *Encyclopedia of Bible Words*, exposes the human capacity to violate the moral standards established by God. *Hata'* means "to miss," and thus fall short of the standard. *Pesa'*, usually translated "rebellion" or "transgression," means to revolt against the standard. And *'awon*, typically translated "iniquity" or "guilt," means to deviate from the standard (page 568).

The New Testament uses two major Greek word-groups that build on the Old Testament view of sin. The first, *'hamartia*, while used in the Septuagint to translate all three of the Hebrew terms, is closest in meaning to *hata'*. It portrays human beings as flawed so that they fail to attain the standard set by God. The second, *'adikia*, which means "unrighteousness" and is often translated "injustice" or "wrongdoing," "focuses attention on conscious human actions which cause harm to other persons in violation of God's standards" (page 567). This second word for *sin* overlaps the biblical concept of evil as a violation of God's intentions that also causes harm.

Taken together, the biblical concepts of sin and evil remind us that the standards God sets are expressions of His love and of grace. To live by the standards protects us and others from the harm that necessarily results from violating them—not because God steps in personally to punish sins, but because in the real world to violate the standards sets in motion consequences that will result in distress, pain and suffering.

There is one more aspect to the relationship between sin and evil. It has to do with the effect of sin and evil on the one who performs them. A biblical example will help define it.

The Effect on the Victimizer

The prophet Habakkuk is deeply disturbed. Godly King Josiah has led a national revival, restored Temple worship and eliminated the hilltop shrines—the "high places"—where the people of Judah had worshiped pagan gods. Despite all that Josiah has done, Jewish society remains riddled with injustice. How can God, who is holy, stand by and witness such evils in His people's lives?

Bringing the question to God, the prophet is shown a stunning vision. At that very moment God is preparing the Chaldeans (the Babylonians) to invade Judah. The revelation actually relieves Habakkuk. God intends the invasion as discipline. Surely He will use it to restore righteousness among His people.

But then Habakkuk has another thought. The Babylonians, known for their cruelty and rapacious ways, are more wicked than the people of Judah. When the Babylonians devastate little Judea they will credit their power for the conquest, never realizing that they have been God's agents. How could God use a more wicked nation to punish His people without making them pay a price for their evil deeds?

In chapter 2 of the little book of Habakkuk, God speaks to His puzzled prophet and gives him a surprising answer. Briefly, God shows Habakkuk that the wicked only seem to get away with doing evil. *Evil has consequences for the victimizer as well as the victim!*

As chapter 2 develops, God lays out several psychological and interpersonal consequences of doing evil that have impact on the evildoer even as he or she appears most successful. Briefly, three of the psychological and interpersonal consequences of doing evil developed in this chapter are:

1. Dissatisfaction	The wicked will never be satisfied.
2. Vulnerability	The wicked person arouses hostility.
3. Insecurity	The wicked can never be secure.

A similar insight is expressed in Isaiah 57:20–21, where the prophet writes, "The wicked are like the tossing sea, which cannot rest, whose waves cast up mire and mud. 'There is no peace,' says my God, 'for the wicked.'"

Each of these passages reflects a psychological reality rooted in the theological concept of evil. Wicked actions necessarily have consequence, harming victim and victimizer alike. Understanding this aspect of the theological concept of evil provides a counselor or a minister with an important tool to bring to his or her ministry.

A Modern Case Study

The relationship between sin and evil is a close one, for God's standards of right and wrong lay out options that either benefit the one who obeys the standards, as well as others, or cause harm to the one who violates the standards, as well as others.

Let's look at an example of how this works in the Christian counseling arena.

Helen, a 56-year-old woman, comes to you with a cluster of complaints. She has been sleeping poorly, and has been feeling a lot of anxiety. She finds herself checking the door a dozen times a night to make sure it is locked. Just the other night she got out of bed three times to make sure she had locked it. She has quite a lot of money and is deeply upset about the economy. She has changed banks three times in the last two months. She is also upset about her relationship with her younger sister, Ann. She and Ann used to be close, but now they rarely speak to each other. Helen says it is as though there is a wall between them.

Looking Deeper

Helen's complaints are not all that unusual. Any experienced pastor or counselor will realize that there are a number of possible causes of Helen's problems. But unless the counselor has some insight into the theological concept of evil, he or she is unlikely even to consider the possibility that Helen may be experiencing consequences of something she has done. And if her complaints are rooted in evil actions, it is even more unlikely that the treatment offered by the counselor will do anything more than reduce the strength of the symptoms while leaving the root problem unresolved.

This, of course, is the point. Now, we should not assume that every complaint a person has is caused by evil actions on his or her part. I simply suggest that unless a pastor or counselor has some insight into the impact of evil on *victimizer* as well as on *victim*, a possible cause of psychological disturbance may be overlooked or ignored. In cases where dissatisfaction, anxiety and insecurity are rooted in evil deeds, failure to diagnose the cause will make it impossible to treat the client effectively. Later we will see that more is at stake in recognizing the nature and impact of evil than we might imagine.

Chances are that if Helen goes to a psychiatrist, she will come away with prescriptions for Ambien to help her sleep and Lexipro to reduce her anxiety. If she goes to a counselor who is a behaviorist, she will learn techniques for reducing the frequency of the "door checking," and develop a bedtime routine designed to help her get to sleep. A different counselor might help her analyze patterns in her conversations with Ann, and suggest ways to reduce the perceived distance. But few counselors would consider the possibility that Helen's problems might be rooted in sin or evil.

Scripture portrays evil both as acts that harm others and as the actual harm—the distress, pain and troubles—that evil acts cause. We noted above that evil actions also cause psychological and interpersonal damage to the victimizer as well as the victim. With this in view, a counselor who takes Scripture's portrait of reality seriously would at the very least be open to the possibility that Helen's complaints are a consequence of some evil she has done.

The Real Source of Pain

When talking with Helen, her counselor discovered that her presenting symptoms emerged a little over eighteen months previously. Exploring what was happening in Helen's life about that time, the counselor learned that about two years ago Helen had a brief affair with Ann's husband. Not long after the affair ended, Ann initiated a divorce. Although Ann's husband had been unfaithful almost from the beginning of the marriage, Helen worried that she was responsible for the breakup of her sister's marriage.

Helen's counselor, a Christian, realized that Helen had to deal with the sin. She led Helen, also a believer, to acknowledge the relationship as sin, to confess the sin to God and to welcome the forgiveness offered in Christ.

The counselor also helped Helen face what it might take to be reconciled with her sister. The counselor pointed out that where sin disrupts a relationship, it is necessary to confess to that person, seek forgiveness and, where possible, make restitution. Helen, while recognizing that her feelings of guilt and shame could be responsible for the distance between herself and Ann, also believed that Ann knew about the affair—or that she was likely to find out. So Helen, fearfully, decided she had to go and speak with Ann, even though she was uncertain how Ann would react.

At each stage in this process the counselor relied on Scripture's portrait of psychological realities. Remember: Doing evil has an impact on the victimizer as well as the victim. Rather than simply try to relieve symptoms, this Christian counselor focused on their root cause. The counselor realized that the primary need of evildoers is to acknowledge and repudiate their sins, to confess them to God and to accept His forgiveness. Then he or she should seek to repair as much as possible any relational breach the evildoing has caused.

This does not mean confession and forgiveness will instantly free Helen from her symptoms, or that the counselor will not use other tools. In Helen's case the counselor gave Helen some practical suggestions for replacing certain patterns of thinking and behavior that had become habitual. But the underlying cause of Helen's distress has been diagnosed and dealt with, and healing will come.

Dealing with Sin and Evil

Helen, in having an affair with her sister's husband, may have set in motion events that led to the breakup of Ann's marriage. And there may be no way to repair that damage. But the affair also did spiritual and psychological damage to Helen. It is important to remember that God has as much love and concern for Helen, the victimizer, as for Ann, who appears to be the chief victim. A counselor should share and express that same love and concern. Judging others is not our role. Our role is to minister to hurting people, to offer them the healing that is found in the atonement.

Some of the damage done by sin and evil can never be repaired. But inner healing for sinners and sinned against alike can be found in the grace of God.

What Ann Did

Sensitive to the Bible's teaching on evil, and aware that the victimizer as well as the victim suffers consequences from evil actions, the counselor saw Helen's symptoms as a possible consequence of her actions and led Helen to acknowledge (confess) her sin to God and accept His forgiveness. This lay the foundation for Helen's healing. But it fell short of dealing with all the consequences of her sin.

Helen feared that her sister knew of the affair and that it had been the cause of the divorce, even though Ann's husband had a history of unfaithfulness. So Helen decided that she had to confess to her sister as well as to God and seek her forgiveness. Helen's tearful confession was angrily rejected by Ann, and only later did the counselor discover the tangled web of sins that Helen's affair had unleashed.

Ann did know about the affair, as Helen feared. When Ann discovered it, she was consumed with anger. Ann had been jealous of her popular older sister as a child, and deeply hurt by her husband's continuing unfaithfulness. All these emotions surged out of control when Ann learned of Helen's betrayal. Enraged, Ann initiated a divorce from her husband, never letting him know she was aware of his infidelity with her sister.

Ann also determined to take revenge on Helen. Ann, trained as an accountant, had power of attorney over their aged parents' estate. Knowing how concerned Helen was with money, Ann took steps to defraud Helen of her share of the estate. In the meanwhile, she pretended ignorance of Helen's affair, although she could not entirely hide her feelings from Helen, who sensed the growing distance between them.

The evil that Helen had done caused Ann that harm, distress and misery implicit in the *ra'* root. But Helen's evil action generated even more evil in Ann, who in her pain planned to do evil in return. Evil begets evil. And when it does, our lives become more and more tangled in a web of sins and misery.

The Way Out

There is only one way to break this chain of evil between Helen and Ann. Ann must come to the point at which she is willing to acknowledge her revenge as sin. The anger she feels is understandable and valid. It is appropriate in view of the sins committed against her. But Scripture tells us: "In your anger do not sin" (Ephesians 4:26). When anger pushes us to take revenge, sin gains a grip on our lives. Scripture says,

> Do not repay anyone evil for evil. Be careful to do what is right in the eyes of everybody. If it is possible, as far as it depends on you, live at peace with everyone. Do not take revenge, my friends, but leave room for God's wrath, for it is written: "It is mine to avenge; I will repay," says the Lord.
>
> Romans 12:17–19

Ann needs to deal both with the evil she has experienced and the evil she has done. The first step is to acknowledge (confess) her sin to God, and to accept His forgiveness. She needs to surrender her right to take revenge and trust God to deal with her sister's sin, either in forgiveness or judgment. Ann then needs to confess what she has done to Helen and seek her forgiveness. And, of course, Ann needs to make restitution for the financial harm she has done to her sister.

It will take time and effort to repair the damage done to Helen and to Ann, and to rebuild their relationship. Certainly counseling can help. But, as I noted earlier, only a counselor with an appreciation for and understanding of Scripture's teaching on sin, evil and forgiveness can hope to reach this point.

The Evil Underneath

Thus far in this study, we have looked at the nature of evil, at the role of Christian counseling in healing the impact of evil on the victimizer and at healing the impact of evil on the victim. In a paradigm suggested by Charles H. Kraft, what we were doing was "clearing away the garbage." In Kraft's view, while clearing away the garbage is the first and perhaps most important phase of healing, there is more to be done.

Most counselors who operate from a distinctively Christian perspective would have few problems with the approach I have outlined. They certainly might suggest refinements to my broad outline. But the need to deal with the consequences of evil through confession, accepting and extending forgiveness and wherever possible providing restitution, would likely be affirmed as both biblical and practical. Now, however, we venture far beyond boundaries that most Christian counselors would set. Yet if we are to deal biblically—and practically—with evil, venture we must.

The Testimony of Ephesians

Let's recap what we have learned in the text of this book. In his letter to the Ephesian church, the apostle Paul states that "our struggle is not against flesh and blood, but against the rulers, against the authorities, against the powers of this dark world and against the spiritual forces of evil in the heavenly realms" (Ephesians 6:12).

The city of Ephesus in the first century was a center of both religion and magic. This is clear from Luke's Acts 19 description of Paul's ministry there. It is also clear from the many references in the epistle of Ephesians to "rule and authority, power and dominion" (Ephesians 1:21) as well as rulers, authorities (principalities) and powers (see 6:12). The Ephesians were well aware of the nature of the "spiritual forces of evil" identified by the above "power" words. The spiritual forces were spirit beings, thought to be gods and demons and "shades of the dead," which first-century men and women feared and practiced magic to influence. In Ephesus and throughout the Roman Empire some thirteen different "power" terms were used to identify what the Bible plainly calls demons.

Paul's message to the Ephesians concerning the evil spirits they feared is encouraging. Jesus holds the supreme power in the universe, far above all rule, authority, power and dominion (see 1:21). And God provides those who trust Jesus with spiritual armor to protect them from demonic forces of the spirit world. Jesus provides believers with the authority to cast demons out, which authority Paul uses while in Ephesus (see Acts 19:11–12).

Simply put, Paul takes demons seriously. Nor can we have a full understanding of evil—imperative for Christian counseling—unless we are willing to follow where Scripture leads us, to affirm and to take account of these "spiritual forces of evil." We must never overlook demons, who are evil, and are committed to doing evil—the harmful, the wicked—in order to cause human beings as much evil—distress, misery, pain and suffering—as possible.

But here almost no counselors, including Christian counselors, are ready to go. Indeed, any who might go there risk losing their licenses as counselors.

In the case of Helen and Ann, much was accomplished since, amazingly, both were willing to look at their actions in the counseling setting. Their counselor rightly led each of the two women to acknowledge her sin, to repudiate it, to confess it to God and to accept God's forgiveness. Their counselor led them to forgive each other, and helped them repair as much of the damage they had done to each other as possible. And for those counselors who are willing to look at the issues of sin and evil, this is where the ministry generally concludes.

But the impact of evil on Helen and Ann in all likelihood has not yet been undone. And the reason is demons.

Demonization

The Greek word wrongly translated "demon possessed" in our gospels is more accurately rendered "demonized." This is an important distinction. *Demon possessed* suggests that humans are controlled by an evil spirit. This is true only in the rarest of cases. *Demonized* indicates the presence of one or more demons within the personality, and that the demons *influence* the individual to some extent. Oppression by demons may cause physical disabilities, emotional problems, mental problems, distorted thinking, etc. But to be demonized does not imply that demons control choices or actions.

We would be wrong to say that Helen's affair was a demon's fault. Helen made the choice herself, and she is responsible for it. But it might very well be accurate to say that Helen's attraction to Ann's husband was exaggerated by a demon who pushed her further than she would have otherwise gone. In the same way we have to say that Ann's anger at her sister's betrayal was her own. But demons may have fanned her rage until Ann decided to take revenge by defrauding Helen.

When Helen and Ann confessed their sin and dealt with it in God's way, the grip of any demons in their lives was undoubtedly weakened. But the demons did not necessarily "just go away." Once settled into a person, demons want to stay. They have to be cast out.

This is where few Christian counselors are willing to go. And their hesitation is understandable. Even those who claim to trust the Bible completely shy away from its teaching on demons. And accrediting associations often take a dim view of a "Christian" approach to counseling, to say nothing of any counselor who talks of demons. But talk of demons we must when seeking to deal with evil.

Open Doors to Demons

Demons cannot just enter anyone they please. They require what some call an open door and others identify as legal ground. In general there are four primary doors through which demons gain access to an individual. We discussed these in chapter 19, but I will review them briefly here.

The first, and most common, is trauma—the pain and suffering we experience when others sin against us.

The second most common is sin that we commit—typically knowingly and habitually.

The third and most difficult to deal with is occult involvement, which in essence is consciously inviting contact with an evil spirit.

The final, and also common, door is one opened into our lives by a parent or other person with some valid authority over us. This includes generational or family-line curses.

When counseling a person like Helen or Ann, we have to consider the possibility that their actions (the evil they have done) or their hurts (the trauma and distress they have experienced) have opened the door to one or more demonic beings.

We can see how the first and second doors were thrown open to demonization by Helen and Ann. Helen committed adultery with Ann's husband. Ann, having been sinned against, felt anger that she nurtured into rage and then into sins against her parents and her sister. The chances are very good that demons took advantage of these open doors, and claimed the right to be present in each woman's life.

What Can We Do about Demons?

The time to deal with demons is when, as Kraft says, we have "cleared away the garbage"—the tangled web of hurts and sins and passions that both doing evil and the pain resulting from evil produce.

The reason we deal with sins and hurts first is that when these have been dealt with, we have removed the legal ground the demons may claim for continuing their hold on the individual. This is what Kraft means by "clearing away the garbage." The next step is to cast out the demons.

Exorcism is essentially a simple process. We identify the demons who are present and, in the name of Jesus, with the authority He gives to believers, we command the demons to leave. Since demons are identified by their function, the issues with which the counselor has been dealing provide clues to the demons who are likely to be present.

Thus, in Helen we can expect to find demons of lust and illicit desire, demons of fear and anxiety, and demons of guilt, self-loathing and shame. When addressed and challenged, demons will often speak with the client's voice and when commanded will name additional demons who are present. At other times the demons will speak in the client's mind, and what they say can be relayed to us by the client.

In Ann we would expect to find demons of anger, hatred and revenge, along with demons of self-loathing and self-hatred. Each of these women needs to be freed from the demons if she is to escape the grip of evil as it is unveiled in the Word of God.

Conclusion

We can and should affirm the ministries of pastors who counsel and of professional Christian counselors. At the same time we need to be aware that all too few understand the dynamics of evil, or take evil spirits seriously.

I am convinced after studying the writings of those engaged in "spiritual warfare" and "deliverance ministry" that the Christian Church needs to recover an emphasis on deliverance, not as a major emphasis in teaching or preaching, but definitely as part of a local church's disciple-making and healing ministries.

Secular counselors have many impressive ways to help people deal with their problems. They can help an individual reduce the strength of symptoms and function in the world. But it is Christ alone who can heal. And healing is what we need.

Appendix B

"Live Free Support Group" Lesson Plans

L ive Free Support Groups" help believers apply to their lives the biblical insights we have studied in this book—regarding identity, faith, peace, righteousness and truth—in order to experience freedom in Christ.

Once every other week, meet with friends at your or another member's home. Your purpose is to provide mutual encouragement to live free from a sense of personal inadequacy, free from anxiety, free from bitterness, free from loneliness and free from addictive sins. The basis of these freedoms is laid out in the New Testament book of Ephesians, which is the source of the practical steps you encourage each other to take.

The goal is to provide a warm, informal setting for sharing each person's story, and to let God's Word shape and reshape each person's personal story.

Group Size

Two people can follow the "Live Free" process. Three- or four-person groups are generally better. There is no maximum size, but when your group grows to six or more, it is usually a good idea to divide equally to do the process and prayer time, coming together again to read the affirmations.

Launching

There are no special requirements for getting started. Just you and one or two friends who want to explore the freedom Christ provides along with protection from the devil's schemes. Choose an evening to meet; let the group grow naturally as you invite others.

Another way to launch "Live Free" groups is to arrange for a church or group of churches to sponsor a Freedom Workshop, which is held on Friday evenings and Saturdays. These workshops are available at no cost other than travel and lodging expenses. For further information go to www.freedomworkshop.info/.

The Process

Take time to catch up with each other when you meet. Then launch the simple process.

Each session begins with an activity that will help you identify and share an aspect of your personal stories. This is followed by exposing a strategy Satan uses to make our lives empty and unproductive. You then briefly explore together a truth that exposes Satan's lie and leads to a satisfying, productive life. God's truth is then applied to each person's story through further sharing.

Lift each other up in prayer, and conclude by reading together an affirmation of God's truth and your commitment to live that truth.

Commitments

It helps if each person accepts certain responsibilities to the others:

1. To attend meetings faithfully.
2. To freely share my story.
3. To respect others' stories, and keep what they say confidential.
4. To pray for and encourage each other.
5. To welcome the prayers of the others.
6. To seek God's help to live the truths explored.

Leadership

Let the study guide lead your sharing. Simply follow each step and move on when the group senses it is time.

Session I

Identity

Open with This Activity

Read Luke 15:11–24 privately. Then write a one paragraph description of the lost son. Gather together and read your paragraphs aloud. Talk it over. In what ways were your descriptions similar? In what ways did they differ?

Recognize Satan's Lie

Satan is eager for us to see ourselves as "lost sons," isolated from the Father. All too often we leave our Father and our true home. Too often we take the gifts He gives us and misuse them in "wild living."

Satan wants us to focus on these failures. He tells us we are sinners who are no longer worthy to be called sons. He wants us to hope for acceptance as mere servants. The more we think of ourselves as unworthy, the more we focus on our sins and failures, then the more certain we are to miss the blessings God has prepared for us.

Hear God's Truth

The apostle Paul tells us in the book of Ephesians that "in love [God] predestined us to be adopted as his sons through Jesus Christ" (Ephesians 1:4–5). God does not see us as sinners and failures, although He knows us completely. God sees us as the father in Jesus' story viewed his lost son. We are God's dearly loved children. He has an unshakable love for us: not only a love that makes Him eager to welcome us home when we stray, but a love that, understood, moves us to love Him and serve Him in return.

Respond to God's Truth

Imagine you are the lost son. Tell the story as the son, sharing how the father's welcome makes you feel about yourself and about him.

Affirm This Truth

Read the following affirmation aloud together:

> Father, I confess my failure to see myself as You see me.
> I confess that I have believed Satan's lie;
> I have forgotten that I am a son,
> blessed with every spiritual blessing.
>
> Father, I confess that I am Your child,
> accepted in the beloved.
> I am Your child,
> gifted with Your own indestructible heredity.

Father, bless me with the ability to see myself
as You see me,
that I may glorify You in all that I am
and all that I do. Amen.

Memorize God's Word

Memorize the following Scripture, and quote it together the next time you meet.

How great is the love the Father has lavished on us, that we should be called children of God! And that is what we are! The reason the world does not know us is that it did not know him. Dear friends, now we are children of God, and what we will be has not yet been made known. But we know that when he appears, we shall be like him, for we shall see him as he is. Everyone who has this hope in him purifies himself, just as he is pure.

1 John 3:1–3

Session 2

Faithfulness

Open with This Activity

You will need decks of playing cards and one tennis ball.

Work in pairs to build a five-story house of cards. Each structure must be strong enough to hold up a tennis ball placed on top. Take five to ten minutes to complete the houses of cards.

Think for a minute how you felt just before you tried to build your house of cards. Then share stories of a time in your life you felt much the same way.

Recognize Satan's Lie

Satan wants to convince us that we will never succeed in doing things that are important to us and to the Lord. He wants to destroy our confidence and make us feel hopeless. We each face different life situations. And most of us have some area in which we feel hopeless. We even cry out to God, and yet nothing seems to change. Then Satan's demons say, "See! I told you so. Things will never change. You're a pitiful failure."

Hear God's Truth

The God who loves us and has chosen us, the God who has adopted us into His family as sons with full access to His resources, does not see our situations as we see them. Ephesians 2:10 states that "we are God's workmanship, created in Christ Jesus to do good works, which God prepared in advance for us to do." Since God is faithful, we can trust Him to strengthen us so that our lives and actions will glorify Him. Because God is faithful we can live confidently, certain that He has provided for us "hope and a future" (Jeremiah 29:11).

Respond to God's Truth

Tell a story about one time God was faithful to you. As each tells his story, let an awareness of God's past involvement in your lives fill your hearts with hope.

Pray together, inviting the Holy Spirit to be with you in power. If anyone is struggling with hopelessness or despair, pray for him or her. Rebuke the spirits of hopelessness, despair and depression, and command them to leave. Then bless each person present with renewed trust in God's faithfulness.

Affirm This Truth

Read the following affirmation aloud together:

> O God of Power and Might,
> Father, Son and Holy Spirit,

I worship and praise You, Father,
    all powerful.
I worship and praise You, Jesus,
    name above every name.
I worship and praise You, Holy Spirit,
    who fills with divine power.

O God of Power and Might,
Father, Son and Holy Spirit,
    I confess my feelings of hopelessness.
    I acknowledge that those feelings are not rooted in
      truth.
    I repudiate them as Satan's lies.

O God of Power and Might,
Father, Son and Holy Spirit,
    Your presence in my life guarantees me hope and a
      future.
    I choose to trust You and Your Word.
    I choose to live in hope,
      now and forevermore. Amen.

Memorize God's Word

Memorize the following Scripture, and quote it together the next time you meet.

May the God of hope fill you with all joy and peace as you trust in him, so that you may overflow with hope by the power of the Holy Spirit.

Romans 15:13

Session 3

Identity

Open with This Activity

Picture yourself in a room of your childhood home with one of your parents. Tell the story of something good that happened there.

Then visit that room again. This time tell a story that illustrates bad things that happened to you there.

Recognize Satan's Lie

Few parents are ideal. Most love their children, and do the best they can. But most of us have also been damaged by our parents. Satan eagerly uses their weaknesses and their sins to attack us. And he actively reminds us of incidents when they made us feel guilty or ashamed or unimportant. Satan tries to make these things appear so large that we lose sight of the positives about our childhoods and ourselves. Of course, in too many homes there were few or no positives. Then Satan reminds us of all that we were deprived of as children and urges us to feel resentment and anger, toward our parents and toward God.

Hear God's Truth

God "predestined us to be adopted as his sons through Jesus Christ" (Ephesians 1:5). Male and female, we have been adopted "as His sons." In Roman law an adopted son was severed from his "old" family, and no longer responsible to his birth father. His only family link was to his adoptive father. And he was considered to possess all that his new family possessed.

This is the significance of Paul's statement that God the Father has "blessed us in the heavenly realms with every spiritual blessing" (verse 3). However we may have been damaged by our earthly fathers, we now have a totally new identity. And the resources provided by our Father God are more than sufficient to make up for the failings of our childhood homes. God will provide us with all we need to lead productive and meaningful lives.

Respond to God's Truth

Place one chair in the center and arrange the other chairs around it. Take turns sitting in the center chair. Each person in the circle is to pray for the individual in the center, asking God to provide whatever he or she senses may have been lacking from the person's childhood. Each prayer should conclude: "In the name of God your Father, I bless you with (the needed gift)."

Affirm This Truth

Read the following affirmation aloud together:

> I confess that I have failed:
> > I have failed to understand my identity as an adopted
> > son;
> > I have failed to claim all of my inheritance in Christ;
> > I have failed to live in the victory Christ won for me.
>
> Yet I affirm God's truth:
> > I believe that I have been adopted as a son;
> > I believe that I have been blessed with every spiritual
> > blessing;
> > I believe that in Christ all God's riches are now mine.
>
> I hereby acknowledge my new identity:
> > I forgive any sins my parents committed against me;
> > I claim the victory over any weaknesses of the past;
> > With God's help I will live as the new creation in
> > Christ that I truly am. Amen.

Memorize God's Word

Memorize the following Scripture, and quote it together the next time you meet.

> I can do everything through him who gives me strength.
>
> Philippians 4:13

Session 4

Identity

Open with This Activity

Tell a story about the most hurtful thing anyone has ever said or done to you. Talk the stories over. What made these particular experiences so painful?

Recognize Satan's Lie

Satan uses the sins of others against us. Each hurt becomes a wound that strikes at the heart of who we are. His demons whisper, "If he can do that to you, you must be crap." "If she treats you that way, you must have no worth or value at all."

When we are wounded by others time and time again we can lose our sense of self. We can become ready victims, accepting any blow as something we deserve. We can stop trying, convinced that we will never succeed anyway. We can buy the lie that since no one treats us with respect, we are not worthy of respect. We can come to the place where we are so down on ourselves that the most hurtful things ever said to us are the things we say to ourselves.

Respond to God's Truth

God does not make any junk. Nothing anyone says about you or does to you can change the reality that, as a human being, you are made in God's image. And as a Christian, you are a dearly loved child of God. Satan uses the sins of others against us to plant lies in our hearts. We need to grasp the truth that we are not defined by what others think about us or do to us. We are defined by God.

One of the things that having faith means is to hear the Word of God and to grab hold of that Word, no matter how others make us feel. In time as we hold on to Truth and act on Truth, our feelings change. Feelings are real, but they are not necessarily reality. Reality is defined by God, and we are called to live by God's Truth.

Respond to God's Truth

Meditate individually on 1 John 3:1–3. Invite the Holy Spirit to speak to you as you focus on the verses for 15 minutes. It will help to jot down your thoughts and observations.

How great is the love the Father has lavished on us, that we should be called children of God! And that is what we are! The reason the world does not know us is that it did not know him. Dear friends, now we are children of God, and what we will be has not yet been made known. But we know that when he appears, we shall be like him, for we shall see him as he is. Everyone who has this hope in him purifies himself, just as he is pure.

1 John 3:1–3

Imagine what would have happened if Jesus were with you in the situation you described when the group began. Retell the story as you think it would have been if Jesus were with you then.

Affirm This Truth

Read the following affirmation aloud together:

> As a child of God,
>> I reject Satan's lies about me.
>> I reject the lie that I am insignificant.
>> I reject the lie that I am not worth respect.
>> I reject the lie that I will never amount to anything.
>
> As a child of God,
>> I repudiate feelings that are not in harmony with Truth.
>> I repudiate feelings of inferiority.
>> I repudiate feelings of worthlessness.
>> I repudiate feelings of insignificance.
>
> As a child of God,
>> I commit to live in accord with God's Truth.
>> I will face each day sure of His love for me.
>> I will face tomorrow confident He will enable me.
>> Through Jesus Christ, my Lord, Amen.

Memorize God's Word

Memorize the following Scripture, and quote it together the next time you meet.

> How great is the love the Father has lavished on us, that we should be called children of God! And that is what we are! The reason the world does not know us is that it did not know him.
>
> 1 John 3.1

Session 5

Righteousness

Open with This Activity

Tell a story about giving in to a temptation when you were a young child. After all have told their stories, talk about your experiences. At the time, did you think that giving in was a big thing, or a small thing? Why?

Recognize Satan's Lie

Satan is eager for us to see faults in others while we excuse flaws in ourselves. We criticize another person for telling lies, but gloss over our own tendency to gossip. We condemn the financier who cheats clients out of millions, but overlook the few dollars with which we pad our expense accounts. We feel contempt for the politician whose affair is exposed, but then we watch a pornographic film in a hotel room. Satan assures us that our sins are minor, not worth a second thought. And all the time demons use them as open doors through which they can enter and exercise their influence.

Hear God's Truth

God calls us to live righteous lives. He calls us to put off our old self and our former way of life, and to "put on the new self, created to be like God in true righteousness and holiness" (Ephesians 4:24). A righteous life is like the metal breastplate worn by a Roman legionnaire to protect his vitals. Even "small" sins, if they become habits, make us vulnerable to demonic attack and influence. We are God's dearly loved children, and we are called to live holy lives, as God's own.

Respond to God's Truth

Tell a fictionalized story about a temptation you experience ten years from now, and describe how you will respond. After all have told their stories, talk about them. Why did you pick the particular temptation you chose? Tell why you responded to the temptation as you did.

Affirm This Truth

Read the following affirmation aloud together:

> Father, You have called me to live a righteous life.
> I confess that I have fallen short in many ways.
> I acknowledge my sins and failures.
> I praise You for the forgiveness You have provided
> for me in Christ.
>
> Father, You have called me to live a righteous life.
> I repent of my sins.

I repudiate any evil that is part of my lifestyle.
I praise You for the power to change—
    power that flows into me from Christ Jesus.

Father, I choose righteousness.
    I choose to follow Jesus.
    I choose to honor You in every way.

Holy Father,
    I rely on You to enable me—
    for the sake of and in the name of Jesus. Amen.

Memorize God's Word

Memorize the following Scripture, and quote it together the next time you meet.

And if the Spirit of him who raised Jesus from the dead is living in you, he who raised Christ from the dead will also give life to your mortal bodies through his Spirit, who lives in you.

Romans 8:11

Session 6

Healing

Open with This Activity

Distribute 3" x 5" cards. Have each person talk for four minutes about the strengths and weaknesses of his or her parents.

As each person talks, the others should stay sensitive to the Holy Spirit and jot down any areas in which they sense the speaker might need release from bondage.

Recognize Satan's Lie

Satan takes every opportunity to use the sins or weaknesses of others against us. Satan may, for instance, use a parent who is a perfectionist to cause a child to think he can do nothing right and is a failure. Even well-meant criticism can be used by demons to bring us into bondage. Many of our problems have their origin in just this way, as Satan twists things others do and say to bring us into bondage—whether that bondage is tied to a poor self-image, to resentment of authority, to anger at real or imagined affronts or to whatever. That bondage may have begun in childhood, but Satan wants it to be a lifelong burden.

Hear God's Truth

Satan binds. Jesus sets free. The distorted ideas, the emotions, the reactions that pattern our lives and keep us from experiencing the life Jesus died to provide for us are, at heart, satanic lies. The Bible says this: "It is for freedom that Christ has set us free" (Galatians 5:1). That freedom is not only freedom from legalism, but also freedom from the other forms of bondage Satan has imposed. We can use the spiritual resources that God has provided to break Satan's bonds, and free us from the demons who lurk in the hidden areas of our lives.

Respond to God's Truth

Share any possible areas of bondage each of you sensed as each one shared about his or her parents. If you recognize truth in what others say about your story, stop. Express forgiveness for any role parents have played, and confess any related personal sin. Renounce any evil spirits associated with that area. Another group member should then in Jesus' name command any evil spirits present in the person to leave.

Affirm This Truth

Father,
I thank You that You are a perfect parent—loving, compassionate, strong.

I forgive my parents for any way in which they fell
short of Your example.
I reject any lies Satan may have implanted in my
heart through their failures.
I repudiate now and forever any evil spirits who may
have used their failures to gain influence in my
life.
I commit myself fully to Jesus.
I ask the Holy Spirit to fill me now.
In the name of Jesus, I command any spirits who
have been repudiated to leave me now, and never
to return, Amen.

Memorize God's Word

Memorize the following Scripture, and quote it together the
next time you meet.

When Jesus had called the Twelve together, he gave them power
and authority to drive out all demons and to cure diseases.

Luke 9:1

Dispelling Demons

Open with This Activity

Each of you write down the first three words you think of when you hear the word *demon*.

Discuss. What do you know (or think you know) about demons that led you to write down those particular words? How accurate do you think your view of demons actually is? Why?

Next, each of you write down three feelings you associate with being demonized. That is, if you suddenly discovered that demons were operating in your life, what would your most powerful feelings be?

List the feelings identified by the group. Then talk about why you generated those particular feeling words. What do they tell you about your view of demons?

Recognize Satan's Lie

C. S. Lewis wrote,

> There are two equal and opposite errors into which our race can fall about devils. One is to disbelieve in their existence. The other is to believe, and to feel an excessive and unhealthy interest in them. They themselves are equally pleased with both errors.

Satan is delighted when we focus our attention on demons and find ourselves either fascinated or fearful. The more we concentrate on the demons themselves, the less likely we are to find freedom from them.

Hear God's Truth

The Bible pictures the resurrected Jesus seated at the Father's right hand "far above all rule and authority, power and dominion, and every title that can be given, not only in the present age but also in the one to come" (Ephesians 1:21). Compared to Jesus, demons are weak and pitiful creatures, doomed for eternity and left with nothing but to scramble around like rats in garbage seeking to do whatever harm they can.

The key to getting rid of demons is not to focus on demons. The key is to get rid of what Charles Kraft calls "garbage" in our lives that demons feed on. The garbage serves both as an open door through which demons gain access to us and as the legal basis they claim gives them the right to stay. Once we have gotten rid of the garbage, we can use our authority as God's children to cast the demons out in Jesus' name.

Here is some of the garbage demons exploit to gain access and to maintain a hold on our lives. Beside each "garbage heap" are some of the things we can do to get rid of it.

Garbage Heaps	Shovels
Buried shame, fear, anger and hatred growing out of trauma, hurts	Forgive, repent, give the pain to Jesus
Involvement in the occult	Confess, renounce, forgive self
Associations and environment	Choose friends wisely, leave unhealthy environments
Willful repeated sins	Confess, repent, renounce

When we face such issues, we limit the ability of demons to influence us. And we weaken the grip of any demons who might have gained a foothold. With no basis (legal right) for their presence, demons may simply leave, or can easily be cast out.

Respond to God's Truth

Rather than focus on demons, concentrate on dealing with things in your life that give demons access to you. Pray together, asking the Holy Spirit to show each of you any issues you need to face and to deal with. When the Spirit brings an issue to anyone's mind, pray with that person that the Lord will heal, cleanse or do whatever is necessary to provide freedom.

Affirm This Truth

Jesus, we praise You as resurrected Lord.
  We acknowledge and rejoice in Your supreme position in the universe.
  We acknowledge Your authority over evil and evil spirits.
  We acknowledge Your power to free us.

Jesus, we open our hearts and minds to You—
  who knows us fully and completely, yet has loved us forever.

Purge us of any garbage that clutters our lives.
Make us wholly and fully Your own. Amen.

Memorize God's Word

Memorize the following Scripture, and quote it together the next time you meet.

Get rid of all bitterness, rage and anger, brawling and slander, along with every form of malice.

Ephesians 4:31

Session 8

Dealing with Shame

Open with This Activity

Read this story.

Linda looked at the picture of the girl in the swimsuit with longing and imagined she was just as slim and pretty. She smiled, picturing the way her friends would look at her, especially Josh.

"Linda!"

Mom was calling.

"I need you down here."

Linda got up reluctantly. As she opened her bedroom door Linda caught a glimpse of herself in the hall mirror, and her dream shattered. Suddenly Linda's face was burning. She was not slim and pretty at all. She was dumpy and ugly. And she was filled with shame.

As a young person were you ever ashamed of some feature of your body? What was it, and how did that affect you? Share about this.

Have you ever done something that you were ashamed of? How did that affect you? How did it affect your relationship with others? With God? Share about this.

Recognize Satan's Lie

Of all the emotions demons use to keep us in bondage, one of the most powerful is shame. While guilt involves awareness that we have violated one of our own or of God's moral standards, shame involves fear of rejection by others. Linda feels that her looks arouse contempt rather than admiration, and she feels shame. There are other causes of shame. When we violate moral standards we try to hide what we have done, not so much from fear of punishment as from fear of what other people might think of us if they knew. Down deep we wonder how anyone who knew what we have done could accept or love us.

At this point Satan and his demons take delight in assuring us that what we have done is so terrible no one who knows could possibly accept or love us. The message, pounded into our hearts and minds again and again, is that we are too wicked to be loved, too contemptible to be accepted by any decent person.

The demons tell us that we have to bury what we have done; we have to hide it deep within us and desperately try to ignore it or forget it. The demons know that, buried there, the thing that brings us shame will fester until all our feelings about ourselves are colored by the conviction that we are so unlovable and unacceptable that we dare not reach out for a close, personal relationship with anyone. Anyone who "really knew what we are like" would be as repelled as we are ashamed.

184

Hear God's Truth

God knows us completely. He knows our inmost thoughts and feelings. He is fully aware of everything we have done or contemplated doing. The things in our lives that we are most ashamed of, that we have struggled the hardest to suppress, are not hidden from him. And yet God loves us. And He tells us that we are worth loving, for Christ died to pay for our sins so that God might have a personal relationship with us.

The Gospel reminds us that our worth and value do not depend on what we do or do not do. The Gospel teaches us that despite the worst that we have done, God has chosen us to be members of His family, and with that choice has committed Himself to us totally. In Christ, God has forgiven our sins and our failures. As He announced through the prophet Isaiah, "Though your sins are like scarlet, they shall be as white as snow" (Isaiah 1:18).

What Satan wants us to suppress, God invites us to bring to Him, openly and honestly, that we might be freed from the burden. "If we confess our sins," Scripture tells us, "he is faithful and just and will forgive us our sins and purify us from all unrighteousness" (1 John 1:9).

Experiencing God's love and forgiveness is the first step in our healing. And as we continue to experience God's love we begin to lose the fear that others will reject or condemn us. We learn that we can take the risk of sharing with others, and, in the community of faith, we begin to realize that we truly are loved and are accepted for ourselves.

Respond to God's Truth

How hard was it for you to accept the truth that God loves you completely and unconditionally? What made it most difficult?

How large a role has shame played in your life? Where are you now on your journey of release from the impact of shame?

Pray together, and thank God for the forgiveness that cleanses from sin and releases you from the grip of shame.

Affirm This Truth

> I am loved.
> I have been chosen by the Father.
> I am accepted.
> I have been cleansed by blood of the Son.
> I am healed.
> I have been empowered by the Spirit.
> Loved,
> > accepted,
> > > healed.
> My guilt and my shame are gone,
> > and I am a new creation in Christ Jesus.

Memorize God's Word

Memorize the following Scripture, and quote it together the next time you meet.

God demonstrates his own love for us in this: While we were still sinners, Christ died for us.

Romans 5:8

Larry Richards is a retired graduate school professor who has written some 250 books. He currently lives in North Carolina with his wife, Sue, who is also a writer and speaker. In addition to writing, Larry conducts Freedom Workshops, teaching on the concepts in this book, and writes the blog www.demondope .com.

If you would like to schedule a Freedom Workshop in your church or community, you may contact Larry by email at ancient1 @nc.rr.com.